SAKE

A beyond-the-basics guide to
**UNDERSTANDING, TASTING,
SELECTION & ENJOYMENT**

John Gauntner
Ushihara Mayumi

装　　幀＝寄藤文平　杉山健太郎

＊本書は Stone Bridge Press から 2014 年に発行された『SAKE CONFIDENTIAL』を改訂し、日英対訳版にしたものです。

Originally published in English as Sake Confidential: A Beyond-the-Basics Guide to Understanding, Tasting, Selection and Enjoyment by Stone Birdge Press, Berkeley, California USA. ©2014 John Gauntner. Used by permission of Stone Bridge Press.

日本の酒
SAKE

A beyond-the-basics guide to
UNDERSTANDING, TASTING,
SELECTION & ENJOYMENT

John Gauntner
ジョン・ゴントナー＝著

Ushihara Mayumi
牛原眞弓＝訳

前書き

　日本のお酒は、世界中で人気が高まっている。ワインに追いつくにはまだ長い道のりがあるものの、**通(つう)の飲み物になりつつある**のはたしかで、世界中で知られ楽しまれている。

　統計によれば輸出高が着実に伸びているし、各国のメディアの注目も明らかにそれを示している。ところが、お酒はまだ海外の人々にはあまりよく理解されていない。いや、**じつは日本のふつうの消費者もよくわかっていないのだ！**

　だが今日では、お酒についての基本的な情報は簡単に手に入るようになった。インターネットで調べればすぐに基礎知識が見つかるので、それさえ読めば自信を持って出かけていき、飲んでみることができる。また、お酒を出したり売ったりする世界中の店のほとんどが、お客に学んでもらうのに適した、少なくとも表面的な教育プログラムを持っているものだ。

　だから、お酒について最も基本的な知識を学ぶのはやさしい。そういう情報はどこでも手に入るからだ。ところが、**基本を越えてさらに進もうとすると**、世の中にはあまり情報がない。本書が伝えようとしたのは、まさにそういう情報——基本を越えてはいるが、重要な情報——なのだ。

Preface

Sake is growing in popularity all over the world. While it still has a long way to go to catch up with wine, it is certainly **on its way to becoming a connoisseur beverage** that is known and enjoyed all over the world.

Statistics show steady growth in exports, and media attention everywhere clearly show this. However, sake is still not all that well understood by people outside of Japan, and in truth **by average Japanese consumers either**!

However, these days, basic information on sake is very easy to get. A quick internet search will lead to the basics of sake, just enough to go out and try some with confidence. And most places that serve or sell sake around the world have at least a perfunctory education program in place to help educate their customers.

So it is eay to learn the most basic things about sake as that information is widely available. However, **if we go beyond the basics**, there is not much information out there. It is precisely that kind of information—just beyond the basics but still important—that this book tried to convey.

Preface 前書き

　これは大切なことだと思う。お酒を愛するわたしたちには、日本酒がもつ秘められた魅力と興味深い特徴の多さ、幅広さや奥深さは、ワインや、ほかの文化的な飲み物の世界に負けないということを世の中に伝える義務があるからだ。またお酒は、和食など、日本のほかの伝統的なものに劣らず魅力的で、日本文化を伝えるものなのである。

　日本に住む日本人は、**お酒大使の第一線**である。今日、そしてこれからもずっと、世界中からたくさんの人々が日本を訪れるだろう。その人たちの多くが当然お酒に興味を持ち、多くの疑問を持つ。わたしたちはその疑問に対して、はっきりと、完璧に、そしてもっと日本酒に興味を持ってもらえるように答えられなければいけない。

　わたしの本の対訳版である本書が、その目的を果たす一助になれば幸いである。また、ここで述べた**話題**の多くは、**ほかでは読めないようなもの**なので、楽しんでもらえることと思う。なかの2、3の話題については、頑固な意見を持っている人々もいて、そういう人たちは物事の両面を話すとは限らない。だが本書では、いつも両方の面を示すよう努めた。最終的には、読者の皆さんに自分で判断していただきたい。

　わたしが日本にやってきたのは1988年だが、はじめはあまりお酒に興味がなかった。でも数ヵ月後、ある同僚がおいしいお酒を教えてくれて、わたしの人生は一変したのだ。お酒で身を立てようとか、お酒のプロになろうとかいう意思はまるでなかったし、実際、そうしようと試みたこ

This is important because those of us that love sake need to convey to the world that sake has as many nooks and crannies, as many interesting aspects, as much breadth and depth as the world of wine or any other culturally infused beverage. It is just as fascinating, and conveys as much about the culture of Japan as does Japanese cuisine or any other traditional facet of Japan.

Japanese people living in Japan are **the first line of sake ambassadors**. There are now, and will always be, many people coming to Japan from all over the world. Many of them will be naturally interested in sake, and will have many questions. We need to be able to answer those questions clearly, thoroughly, and in a way that promotes even more interest in *nihonshu*.

It is my hope that this bilingual version of my book will help people accomplish this. Also, **as many topics here are not topics one usually can read about**, I hope that it proves to be fun and interesting as well. There are a couple of topics about which some people have strong opinions, and such people may not always present both sides of the story. I have tried here to always present both sides, and ultimately I hope readers will make decisions for themselves.

I arrived in Japan in 1988, but had no real interest in sake at first. Several months later, someone with whom I worked turned me on to some good sake, and my life changed. I really had no intention of making a career or profession out of sake, and in fact, I never really tried to

とはまったくない。ただ、お酒を飲みたかっただけなのだ！

　だが楽しんでいるうちに、当然のように多くの機会が次々と現れ、やがて気がつくと、お酒を世界に紹介するようになっていた。自分でこういう道を選んだという気はしない。むしろ、**この道がわたしを選んだのだ。**

　わたしにとってお酒がもつ特別なもの、つまり大きな魅力のひとつは、その奥深さだ。お酒の造り方、歴史や文化や飲み方、とくに味わい方や香りの嗅ぎ方——お酒にはとてつもない奥深さがあるので、**決して飽きるということがない。**そう、永遠に。

　お酒に対するこの驚異の念が、本書を通して読者の皆さんにどうか伝わるように、また、皆さんが共感して、ほかの人たちにも伝えてくださるようにと願ってやまない。

　ぜひ、お酒を楽しんでいただきたい！

ジョン・ゴントナー

do so. I just wanted to enjoy it!

But as I enjoyed sake, more and more opportunities presented themselves as a matter of course, and I eventually found myself promoting sake to the world. I guess I do not feel that I chose this line of work, **but rather, it chose me**.

To me, the one thing that is special about sake, the one thing that is its great appeal, is its depth（奥深さ）. Be it the way it is made, or its history or culture or the way it is enjoyed, and especially the way it tastes and smells—there is so much depth to sake that **one can never become bored**. Ever.

I hope that this sense of wonder toward sake is something that I can convey through this book, and that all those that read it can sense themselves, and pass on to others as well.

By all means, enjoy sake!

John Gauntner

目次

前書き *4*

Part 1 お酒の基本 *15*

お酒とは？ *16*

酒造りの歴史と工程 *20*

おいしい酒と、ふつうの酒 *22*

米 *26*

精米 *28*

職人の技能 *30*

お酒の等級 *34*

「純米」酒と「純米」酒でないもの *38*

その他の種類のお酒 *42*

日本酒度 *44*

古酒 *46*

温度 *46*

お酒を飲むときの器とガラス製品 *48*

貯蔵 *48*

お酒と料理 *50*

CONTENTS

Preface 5

Part I Sake Basic 15

What Is Sake? 17

The History and Process of Making Sake 21

Good Sake and Less-Good Sake 23

Rice 27

Milling 29

Craftsmanship 31

The Grades of Sake 35

Junmai Types and Non-*junmai* Types 39

Other Types of Sake 43

The *Nihonshu-do* 45

Aging Sake 47

Temperature 47

Vessels and Glassware for Enjoying Sake ... 49

Storage 49

Sake and Food 51

Part 2 日本酒の秘密 53

1. 「純米」と「純米」でない酒 54
2. 生酒 66
3. 古酒 80
4. 日本酒度 92
5. 吟醸 104
6. お酒の純粋さ 114
7. 酒瓶の日付と、
   「どのくらいで古いのか？」 126
8. 温めたお酒 136
9. にごり酒 150
10. 特別酒 162
11. 「山廃」と「生酛」...................172
12. 地域性 182

索　引 201

Part 2 Sake Secrets *53*

1. *Junmai* vs. Non-*Junmai* *55*
2. *Namazake* *67*
3. Aged Sake *81*
4. The *Nihonshu-do* *93*
5. *Ginjo* *105*
6. Sake Purity *115*
7. The Date on the Bottle and
   "How Long Is Too Long?" *127*
8. Warm Sake *137*
9. *Nigori* *151*
10. *Tokubetsu* *163*
11. *Yamahai* and *Kimoto* Sake *173*
12. Regionality *183*

Index *201*

Part I

Sake Basic

お酒の基本

お酒とは？

お酒とは、一言でいえば米を醸して造る**アルコール飲料**である。わかりきったことと思われるかもしれないが、重要な点が2つあるので、これから話してみよう。

第一に、**発酵材料**からみると、お酒は米のみで造られる。酒造りの過程で、ほかの穀物や糖分を発酵させることはない。水、酵母、「麹」菌は使われるが、ほかの発酵材料が用いられることはない。

第二に、お酒は**醸造酒**である。ワインのような単発酵酒ではなく、ウィスキーのような蒸留酒でもない。ほかよりもビールに近いが、それでもなお独特な酒である。

お酒のアルコール分は15〜16％で、こくのある赤ワインより少し高いだけだ。これは、自然に生じる20％程度の原酒を水で薄めているからで、味わいを楽しむためである。**アルコール分が高すぎると、ほのかな香りや風味が抑えつけられてしまうからだ。**

日本酒造りには、独特な点が多数ある。ビールは、大麦を麦芽にしたとき——つまり、大麦を湿らせて温め、発芽させたとき——に生じる酵素を使って、大麦のデンプンを糖に変化させて造る。しかし、日本酒

What Is Sake?

In short, sake is **an alcoholic beverage that is brewed from rice**. While this may seem obvious, there are two important points revealed here.

One, in terms of **fermentable materials**, sake is made from rice only. No other grains or sugars are fermented in the sake-making process. While water, yeast, and a mold known as *koji* are used, no other fermentable materials are used.

Two, sake is a **brewed beverage**. It is not a simple fermentation like wine, nor is it a distilled beverage like whiskey. It is closer to a beer than anything else but is nonetheless unique.

Sake's alcohol content is about 15–16 percent, which is only a bit higher than a robust red wine. This is watered down from the naturally occurring 20 percent or so simply for enjoyability, since **the higher alcohol content overpowers subtle aromas and flavors**.

Sake production is unique in many ways. Beer is made by converting starches in barley to sugar using enzymes that arise when the barley is malted—that is, when it is moistened, warmed, and allowed to sprout.

白米から造られる。白米とは、外側の茶色い部分——ぬか——を削り取った米である。つまり、ビールを造るときの大麦のように、米を発芽させることはできない。だが長いデンプン分子を細かく切って、非常に小さな糖分子に変えるには、やはり**酵素**が必要である。この糖分子を酵母菌が食べることで、アルコールと二酸化炭素が発生するからだ。

日本酒の醸造では、「麹」菌（学名：「アスペルギルス・オリーゼ」）から酵素を得る。この菌の**胞子**を、1樽の酒になる米の全量の20～25％にふりかける。すると、麹菌が蒸し米の粒のまわりや中で成長し、必要な酵素を生じる。この酵素が米のデンプンを糖に変えるのである。

ビールの場合、デンプンから糖へ変化させる糖化と、糖からアルコールへ変化させる発酵は、別工程で順次行われる。だが日本酒の醸造では、麹菌のついた米から糖が少しずつ醪（もろみ）の中に流れ込み、同じ場所で同時に、酵母菌がその糖をアルコールに変えていく。

この方法は「**並行複発酵**」と呼ばれ、バランスを取るのがとても難しい。そのおかげで、世にある**非蒸留酒**のなかでも最高レベルのアルコール分が自然の力で生み出される。つまり、さきほど述べた20％である。

Sake, however, is made from white rice, which is rice that has had the brown outer part—the **husk**—milled away. This means that it cannot be malted the way barley is for making beer, but **enzymes** are still needed to chop the long starch molecules into smaller, bite-size sugar molecules. These sugar molecules can be gobbled up by the yeast cells, which then give off alcohol and carbon dioxide.

In sake brewing, these enzymes are provided courtesy of *koji* mold (its scientific name is *Aspergillus oryzae*). The **spores** of this mold are sprinkled on about 20–25 percent of all the rice that goes into a batch of sake, and as this mold grows around and into the grains of steamed rice, it gives off the necessary enzymes, which then convert the starch in the rice into sugar.

In beer, the starch-to-sugar conversion and sugar-to-alcohol fermentation take place separately and sequentially. However, in sake brewing, the moldy rice trickles sugar into the **mash** in the same space and at the same time that the yeast cells convert said sugar into alcohol.

The process is referred to as "**multiple parallel fermentation**" and represents a difficult balance to strike. It yields the highest naturally occurring alcohol level of any **non-distilled beverage** on the planet: the aforementioned 20 percent.

🍶 酒造りの歴史と工程

　お酒の歴史はどれくらいか？　端的に答えれば、約1000年である。製造方法と完成品の性質において、**今日我々が飲んでいるようなものになったのは、そんなにも遠い昔なのだ。**

　ところが実際には、なんと1700年ほど前にも、お酒はあった。当時、置きっぱなしの蒸し米の上に「麹」菌が自然発生し、さらに酵母が落ちて、オートミールのようにどろどろの酒ができたのだ。

　しかし高級な「吟醸」酒のように、**洗練された香り高い酒が、**商品として市場に出回るようになったのは、ここ40年ほどのことである。「吟醸」以前の酒が劣っていたというわけではない。「吟醸」ほど華やかではないが、同じくらいおいしいものだった。

　お酒を造るには、秋に収穫した米を精米し、水につけてから蒸す。その蒸し米の約4分の1に「麹」菌を繁殖させる。次に、小さな桶に「麹」米、ふつうの蒸し米、水、酵母を入れて、**酒母**(しゅぼ)(「酛」(もと)ともいう)を造る。ここに酵素菌が密集して繁殖する。これを造るのは、たとえ野生酵母や細菌が貯蔵タンクに入っても、**適正な酵母が豊富にあれば、悪い作用が起きないからだ。**

The History and Process of Making Sake

How long has sake been around? The short answer is about a thousand years. It has been about that long since sake **came to resemble what we enjoy today**, in both production methods and in the nature of the completed product.

But in reality, sake has been around for about 1,700 years. Back then, someone left some steamed rice lying around, upon which naturally occurring *koji* mold and yeast fell. That led to an oatmeal-like, mash-like sake.

Premium *ginjo* sake, however, with all its **refined complexity and aromatic style**, has only been on the market as a viable product for about forty years. This is not to imply sake was a lesser beverage before *ginjo*; not at all. It was just as good, if less ostentatious.

To make sake, rice harvested in the fall is milled, then soaked and steamed. *Koji* mold is grown on about a quarter of it. Next, a **yeast starter** (*moto*) is created in a small vat from a mixture of the *koji* rice, regular steamed rice, water, and yeast. Here a very high concentration of yeast cells develops. This is to ensure that when wild yeast or bacteria drop into the tank, **the correct yeast will be so abundant that there will be no adverse effects**.

この小さな酒母に、さらに多くの「麴」米、蒸し米、水を、4日間にわたって、酵母の数が減りすぎないよう3回に分けて加える。この混合物――どろどろの状態で、「醪」と呼ぶ――を、約20〜40日間発酵させる。それから、溶けきれなかった米の粕を濾して取り除く。それがすむと、出来上がったばかりの酒は**低温殺菌**され、濾過され、伝統的には6ヵ月貯蔵される。そのあと**水**で少し薄め、再び低温殺菌し、瓶詰めする。

　これが酒造りの大筋である。初めから終わりまで、製造に6〜8週間、その後の熟成に約6ヵ月かかる。とはいえ、変種や例外も数えきれないほどある。

おいしい酒と、ふつうの酒

　率直に言おう。今では、市場に出ている酒にまずいものはほとんどない。適切に製造されたもので、失望させられることはないだろう。だがもちろん、ふつうの酒になったり、すばらしい酒になったりする要因はある。
　しかしその話をするまえに、お酒がぐっと身近になる考え方を紹介しよう。だれもが賛成するというわけではないが、わたしは支持している。それは、日

To this small yeast starter, more *koji* rice, steamed rice, and water are added at three different times over four days to keep the yeast population from thinning out too much. This mixture—the mash or *moromi*—is allowed to ferment for about twenty to forty days, then the **rice lees** that did not completely liquefy are filtered away. After that, the just-completed sake will be **pasteurized**, filtered, and stored, traditionally for six months. Then **it is diluted a bit**, pasteurized again, and bottled.

This is the gist of the process. From start to finish, it takes six to eight weeks for production, then about six months for **maturation**. But there are countless variations and exceptions.

Good Sake and Less-Good Sake

Let's face it: there is almost no bad sake out there anymore. Nothing properly cared for will make you cringe. There are, of course, **factors that make one sake good but another great**.

However, before we get to that, here is a concept that makes sake extremely approachable. While not everyone will completely agree with this, I stand by

本酒の価格は90％の確率で適正であり、**支払っただけの値打ちがある**ということだ。もちろん、お酒の好みがはっきりしているなら——つまり好きな銘柄が決まっているなら——、値段よりも好みを優先して決めればいい。だが、どれが好きかわからない場合、または目の前に知らない酒ばかり並んでいる場合には、値段をもとにして選べば90％の確率で間違いがない。

例外はあるだろうか？　もちろんある。**何事にも例外があるのは、お酒の世界でも同じだ**。品質のわりに高すぎる酒があれば、お買い得の酒もある。しかしそういうものは、おそらく10本に1本である。だから90％の確率で、値段をもとに決め、安心して購入し、選んだ酒をゆっくり楽しむことができる。

さらに、瓶のどこかに「吟醸」という文字のあるものを常に飲むようにすれば、最高級の酒をいつも味わうことができるだろう。

さて次に、日本酒の価格が90％の確率で適正であることを踏まえて、**価格と品質に何が影響しているのか**考えてみよう——ある酒が比較的安くてふつうの味になり、別の酒は非常に高価で、天国の飲み物のような味と香りがするようになる、その要因は何だろう？

手短に言えば、価格と品質に影響するものは3つある。それは米、精米、職人の技術である。

it: 90 percent of the time, sake is fairly priced, and **you will get what you pay for**. Naturally, if your preferences in sake are clear—if you know what you like—then defer to those rather than price in making a decision. But should you not know what you like, or anything about the selections before you, making a decision based on price will work 90 percent of the time.

Are there are exceptions? Of course. **There are exceptions to everything in the sake world**. There are sake that are overpriced and sake that are deals. But these will make up perhaps one bottle out of ten, so 90 percent of the time you can make a decision based on price, feel safe about it, then relax and enjoy the sake you have chosen.

Furthermore, if you always drink sake with the word *ginjo* somewhere on the bottle, you will always enjoy sake that is ensconced in the realm of the super premium.

Next, since sake is fairly priced 90 percent of the time, let's consider **what affects price and quality**—what it is that makes one sake relatively inexpensive and mundane, while another is quite pricey and tastes and smells like ambrosia from heaven?

In short, there are three things that affect price and quality: rice, milling, and craftsmanship.

米

　いいワインが、食料品店で買う葡萄とはまったく違う葡萄から造られるように、いい日本酒も、**ふつうに食べる米とはまったく違う米から造られる**。すべての日本酒が正規の酒米から造られるわけではないので注意しよう。しかし、高級な酒はほとんどが酒米を原料としている。

　酒米と普通米には、いくつかの違いがある。酒米は普通米より稲の背が高く、粒が約30％大きく、**デンプンが多くて脂肪とタンパク質が少ない**。また、まず糖に変化し、それからアルコールへと変化するデンプンが、一粒一粒の中心部に集中している。そのデンプンを包むように米粒の表面近くにあるのが、脂肪とタンパク質である。

　普通米ではこれらは米粒の中で混じり合っており、色も全体にかなり均一である。脂肪、タンパク質、デンプンがもっと均等に配置されているからだ。しかし酒米では、**デンプンの集まった白い中心部のある米粒が多い**。そして脂肪とタンパク質はそのまわりの部分、つまり米粒の表面に近い半透明のところにある。これには重要な意味がある。このような構造の米は、表面近くにある脂肪とタンパク質を取り除いて、必要なデンプンだけをあとに残すよう、**効果的に**

Rice

Just as good wine is made from grapes that are quite different from those we buy at the grocery store, good sake is made from **rice that is significantly different from rice that we eat**. Note that not all sake is made from proper sake rice; however, almost all premium sake is.

There are a handful of differences between sake rice and regular rice. Sake rice plants are taller, and the grains are about 30 percent larger and with **more starch and less fat and protein** than regular rice. Furthermore, the starch that will be converted into sugar, and subsequently into alcohol, is physically concentrated in the center of each grain. Surrounding that, near the surface of the rice grain, are fat and protein.

In regular rice, these are more mixed up within the grain, and the color is pretty much uniform throughout because the fats, proteins, and starches are more evenly distributed. But **in sake rice, we can see a white center in many of the grains where the starch is concentrated**. The fat and protein are located in the surrounding, more translucent region closer to the surface of the grain. This is significant because rice constructed this way **can be milled**

精米することができるからだ。

　この中身の違いのせいで、食用の米は酒米よりもおいしいのである。酒米は食べようと思えば食べられるが、約3倍の値段なのに食用の米ほどおいしくはない。

　ワインの原料の葡萄のように、酒米にもさまざまな種類がたくさんある。そしてどの種類にも**独自の特徴と品質レベル**があるので、出来上がる酒にもさまざまな味と香りが生じるのだ。また、これも葡萄と同じだが、それぞれの酒米には、**成長するのに適した地域や天候**がある。しかし（ワインの葡萄と違って）合法的かつ容易に、酒米は育った場所から、国内の醸造者（杜氏）のもとへ送られて使用される。

精米

　高価な酒になる要因の2つ目は、米がどれくらい精米されたかということだ。なぜこれが重要なのだろう？

　上述したように、適正な酒米では、発酵するデンプンが米粒の中心部にある。そのまわりにある米粒の外側に近い部分は、脂肪とタンパク質である。これはつまり、米を精米すればするほど、不要な脂肪とタン

more effectively so as to remove the fat and protein hovering near the surface, leaving only the desirable starch behind.

These differences in content make table rice taste better than sake rice. While you can eat sake rice if you want to, it is about three times as expensive as table rice, and it does not taste as good.

Just like grapes for wine, there are many different varieties of sake rice, all with their **own character and levels of quality**, and these lead to different flavors and aromas in the final sake. Again like grapes, different varieties of sake rice have **regions and climates in which they thrive**. However, sake rice can legally and easily be shipped around Japan for use by brewers (*toji*) in regions other than where it was grown.

Milling

The second thing that makes one sake better and more expensive than another is how much the rice has been milled. Why is this important?

As explained above, in proper sake rice, the starches that will ferment are physically located in the center of the grain. Around that, near the outer portion of the grain, are fats and proteins. This means

パク質を多く取り除くことができるので、必要なデンプンを簡単に手に入れられるということだ。それどころか、大ざっぱにいうと──多くの例外もあるが──、醸造前に**米を精米すればするほど、お酒はおいしくなる**のだ。もちろん精米率を上げるとコストがかかる。同じ量の酒を造るのに、より多くの米が必要になるからだ。しかし、**結果的にはそうする価値がある**。

米を精米する割合は、「精米歩合」(「せいまいぶあい」と発音する)と呼ばれ、精米後に残った米の、**元の大きさに対する割合**で表す。もし「精米歩合」60％と記載されていれば、それは醸造前に、元の大きさのたった60％になるまで米が精米されたという意味である。(つまり、外側の40％は削り取られて、醸造過程では使用されなかったということだ)。

職人の技能

おいしく高価な酒になる要因の3つ目は、酒造りに注がれる**激しい労働と手作りの苦労**である。言いかえれば、機械で造るか、人の手で造るかだ。おそらく日本酒の80％は自動化された工程で製造されており、その多くが申し分ないもので、お酒として十分に

that the more we mill the rice, the more we remove the less desirable fat and protein, and the more easily we can access the sought-after starch. In fact, a great generalization—with plenty of exceptions—is that **the more you mill the rice** before brewing, the better the sake will be. Of course, more milling drives costs up, since you need more rice to get the same job done, but **it is worth it in the end**.

The amount that the rice has been milled is referred to as the *seimai-buai* (pronounced "say my booh eye") and is expressed as **a percentage of the grain's original size** that remains after milling. If the *seimai-buai* is listed as 60 percent, that means the rice was milled before brewing so that only 60 percent of the original size of the grains remained (i.e., the outer 40 percent was ground away and was not used in the brewing process).

Craftsmanship

The third thing that makes one sake better and more expensive than another is the **labor-intensive, hand-crafted effort** that has gone into making it. In other words, sake can be made by machine or by hand. Perhaps 80 percent of sake is made using automated

楽しめる。だが、ほぼ例外なく、**最高品質の酒は手作りである。**

　酒造りの各工程は次の工程の基礎となり、どの工程の成功も、それまでの全工程の出来具合に大きく左右される。だから、はじめに**丹精込める**ことで得られた品質は、最後まで持ち越されるのだ。米の洗い方、漬け方、蒸し方が、「麴」造りに影響し、「麴」造りが今度は発酵に影響するというように、この連鎖が製品の出来上がりまで続くのである。

　では、少し振り返ってみよう。おいしく高価な酒になる3つの要因は、
　米　：よい酒米は高価だが、その値打ちがある。
　精米：一般に、米を精米すればするほど酒の品質
　　　　は上がる。
　労力：多くの場合、人の手で労力と技術を費やす
　　　　ことによって、おいしい酒ができる。

processes, and much of this sake is just fine and can be very enjoyable. However, almost without exception, **the best sake is made by hand**.

Each step of the sake-making process becomes the foundation for the next, and the success of any step depends hugely on **all that has come before it**. So, quality resulting from **painstaking effort** early on is carried through to the end. How the rice is washed, soaked, and steamed affects the *koji* making, which in turn affects the fermentation, and this chain continues until the product is complete.

In review, then, the three things that make one sake better and more expensive than another are:

- Rice: Good sake rice is expensive, but worth it.
- Milling: Generally, the more the rice is milled, the higher the quality of sake.
- Labor: More often than not, hand-crafted, labor-intensive techniques lead to better sake.

🍶 お酒の等級

次ページのイラストは、日本酒の等級の名称と、法的な定義が一目でわかるように示したものである。「川の流れ」を上にいくほど、酒の等級が上がり、価格も高くなる。また、その等級の名称に見合うためには、精米歩合も高くなければならない。

高級酒の等級の名称(「純米酒」、「本醸造酒」、「純米吟醸酒」、「純米大吟醸酒」、「大吟醸酒」)はすべて、**醸造前に米がどれだけ精米されたかによって、「法的に」**定義されているにすぎない。それほど精米は重要なのだ。

お酒についてできるだけ簡単に知りたければ、次のように考えるとよい。もし等級の名称をひとつだけ覚えるなら、「吟醸」にしよう。**吟醸**酒は、シングル・モルト・スコッチがスコッチの代表であり、100％アガーベのテキーラがテキーラの代表であるように、**日本酒の代表である**。成分は同じだが、よりよい製品にするために、**いい原材料と厳密な手法**を使って造られている。瓶のどこかに「吟醸」という文字のある日本酒をつねに選ぶようにすれば、いつも安心して飲むことができる。

ただ、高級酒の名称は重複するものが多いので注意が必要だ。また、味見しただけでその酒がどの等級になるかわかる人は、ほとんどいないということも注意してほしい。

The Grades of Sake

The illustration on the next page shows the grades of sake at a glance, and their legal definitions. The higher up the "river" you go, the higher the grade of sake, the more expensive the sake, and the more highly milled the rice must be to qualify for that grade.

All the grades of premium sake (*junmai-shu* and *honjozo*, *junmai ginjo* and *ginjo*, and *junmai daiginjo* and *daiginjo*) are *legally* defined by little more than **how much the rice was milled before brewing**. That's how important milling is.

To make learning about sake as easy as possible, consider this point: if you remember just one word about the grades of sake, let it be *ginjo*. **Ginjo sake is to regular sake** what single malt scotch is to regular scotch, or what 100 percent agave tequila is to regular tequila. It is the same stuff, but made **with better raw materials and using more exacting methods** to arrive at a better product. If you always drink sake with the word *ginjo* somewhere on the bottle, you will always be in the safe zone.

However, be aware that there is a lot of overlap between the premium grades of sake, and that almost no one can always tell what class a sake belongs to just by tasting it.

The top four grades of sake as a group are referred to as *ginjo-shu* and along with regular *junmai* and *honjozo* make up the six premium sake grades collectively known as *tokutei meishoshu* or "special designation sake."

Namazake, *nigorizake*, *genshu*, *koshu*, and other sake types are available in every grade.

JUNMAI SAKE
Brewed with rice, water, and *koji* (no alcohol added)

Junmai-shu

Tokubetsu Junmai-shu

Seimai-buai (% rice remaining after milling) — 70% or less* — 60% or less

Honjozo-shu

Tokubetsu honjozo-shu

NON-*JUNMAI* SAKE
Brewed with rice, water, *koji*, and a small amount of distilled alcohol

Premium sake

Normal "table" sake

"REGULAR" SAKE
No minimum milling requirement and with larger amounts of alcohol added (65% of the market)

*Seimai-buai for *junmai* sake can exceed 70% but *honjozo* must be 70% or less.

Junmai ginjo-shu

Junmai daiginjo-shu

50% or less

Daiginjo-shu

Ginjo-shu

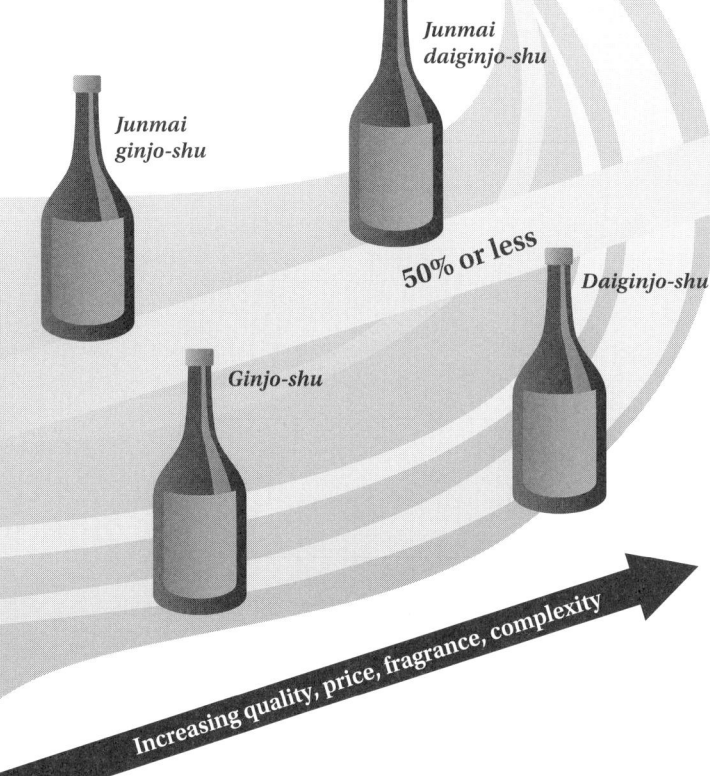

Increasing quality, price, fragrance, complexity

Sake GRADES at a Glance

Futsu-shu

だから、名称について知ってもらいたいが、あまりこだわらないようにしよう。

お気づきかもしれないが、「吟醸」には、さらに4つの分類がある。「純米吟醸」(アルコールを加えないもの)、「吟醸」(アルコールを加えたもの)、「純米大吟醸」(アルコールを加えないもの)、「大吟醸」(アルコールを加えたもの)である。この4つをまとめて「吟醸」と呼ぶ。

「純米」酒と「純米」酒でないもの

川の図の中でいちばん大きな部分は「普通酒」、つまりふつうの(食中用の)酒であることに注目してほしい。これは高級酒ではないが、市場で最も多くの割合を占めている。この種の酒は、価格を下げるために、**かなり多量の純粋蒸留アルコールで薄められている**。注意してほしいのは、これらの酒の多くは本当においしいということだ。だが高級酒ではない。

川の上流にあるいくつかの名称の高級酒は、まとめて「特定名称酒」と呼ばれる。つまり、「特別な名称を与えられた日本酒」ということだ。

その中でも、「純米」という言葉がついている酒は、米、水、「麹」(酵素が豊富な麹米)だけを用いて造られ、アルコールを加えない。

だが、この高級酒のなかで「純米」という言葉を含

So learn the grades, but do not get hung up on them.

You may have noticed that *ginjo* has four subclasses: *junmai ginjo* (which has no added alcohol); regular *ginjo* (which has some added alcohol); *junmai daiginjo* (no added alcohol); and regular *daiginjo* (some added alcohol). All four are collectively known as *ginjo*.

Junmai Types and Non-*junmai* Types

Note that the largest pool in our sake river is labeled *futsu-shu*, or regular (table) sake. This is non-premium sake, and it represents the lion's share of the market. Sake in this realm **has been cut with relatively large amounts of pure distilled alcohol** for economic reasons. Note that a lot of this sake is truly very enjoyable, but it is not premium sake.

The several grades of premium sake shown at the top of the river are collectively known as *tokutei meishoshu*, or "special designation sake."

Among these, anything with the word *junmai* in it is made using only rice, water, and *koji* (the enzyme-rich moldy rice), with no added alcohol.

However, the three sake types within this premium

まない3種類の酒——つまり「本醸造」、「吟醸」、「大吟醸」——は、醸造の最後の行程で蒸留アルコールを加えて造られる。

　この種類の酒では、**卓越した技術的な理由でアルコールを加える**のであって、「普通酒」のように生産量を増やすために加えるのではない。最も大きな理由は、**発酵している醪から香りと味を引き出すため**というものである。醪の中の混合物の多くはアルコールに溶けやすい。発酵が終わってすぐに少量の蒸留アルコールを加えると、全体のアルコール分が高くなるので、より多くの味と香りが引き出されるのだ。ただし、あとで水を加えてアルコール分を通常の16％に下げるので、こういう酒のアルコール分が高いわけではない。製造中の一工程でアルコール分が高くなるだけである。アルコールを加えることには、ほかの利点もある。**製品をなめらかにし、安定性を増し、貯蔵寿命を**のばすという効果がある。

　「純米」酒だけが正当な日本酒だと主張する純粋主義者もいる。だが実際には、どちらかが（「純米」でも「純米」以外でも）、明らかに優れているということはない。

realm that do not include the word *junmai*—i.e., *honjozo*, *ginjo*, and *daiginjo*—are made by adding some distilled alcohol at the end of the brewing process.

In these types, **the alcohol is added for very good technical reasons** and not to increase yields as it is in *futsu-shu* regular sake. These reasons include, most significantly, **helping to extract aromas and flavors from the fermenting mash**. Many of the compounds in the mash are soluble in alcohol; adding a bit of distilled alcohol just after fermentation is complete raises the overall alcohol content, which allows more flavor and aroma to be pulled out. Note that water is later added to bring the alcohol back down to the usual 16 percent so that such sake is not fortified. It just had a higher alcohol level at one stage of its development. Adding alcohol has other benefits too, including **smoothening the product and improving stability and shelf life**.

There are purists who insist only the *junmai* types are valid sake, but in truth, neither type (*junmai* or non-*junmai*) is unequivocally better than the other.

🍶 その他の種類のお酒

　さらに、もう2、3の種類がラベルに表示されていることがある。この表示は名称とは法的に何の関係もなく、あらゆる名称の酒でありうる。

　「にごり酒」は不透明な酒で、**多少の粕を、わざと残してある酒**である。クリーミーで、噛みごたえがあり、豊かな味わいで、何世紀も昔の酒や自家製の酒を彷彿とさせるものだ。

　「生酒」は**低温殺菌しない酒**のことである。新鮮で活力があり、いきいきした味わいだが、低温殺菌した酒よりおいしいとは限らない。

　「原酒」は**水で薄めていない酒**のことで、必ずとは言えないが、たいていアルコール分が高く、だいたい19〜20％である。

　「山廃（やまはい）」と「生酛（きもと）」は、ある方法でこしらえた酒母で造る酒で、通常匂いが強く、味わい豊かで、素朴な味が特徴である。

　「古酒」と「長期熟成酒」は、どちらも熟成させた酒のことである。

　「貴醸酒」は、水のかわりに酒を使って造られる酒である。甘く濃密な味わいのデザート酒だ。生産量は非常に少ない。

　「発泡日本酒」はどうだろうか？　いくつか出回っているが、市場ではかなり新しいもので、炭酸入りの製

Other Types of Sake

Here are a few more types of sake that you may see indicated on a label. These terms have no legal relationship to grade, meaning that these sake types can come in all grades.

Nigorizake is cloudy sake, sake in which **some of the lees have been purposely left behind**. Creamier, chewier, and richer, it is a throwback to sake of centuries past, and to moonshine as well.

Namazake is sake that **has not been pasteurized**. It can be fresh, zippy, and lively, but it is not necessarily better than pasteurized sake.

Genshu is **undiluted** sake, usually but not always of a higher alcohol content, perhaps 19–20 percent.

Yamahai and *kimoto* are styles made with a yeast starter prepared in a way that usually leads to a gamier, richer, earthier flavor profile.

Koshu and *choki-jukuseishu* both refer to aged sake.

Kijoshu is sake made using already completed sake in place of some water. It is a sweet, rich dessert sake. Very little is produced.

What of sparkling sake? There is some out there, but it is relatively new on the market, and a

品の数は希少なほうだ。それなりに楽しめるが、ふつうの日本酒とはまったく別の代物である。

🍶 日本酒度

英語では「サケ・メーター・バリュー」と呼ぶこともあるが、「日本酒度」は酒の比重、つまり、水の密度に対する酒の密度のことである。具体的にいうと、−3と+12の間の数字で表され、その数字が酒の甘さや辛さを示している。**名称や品質とはまったく無関係**だ。

理論上は、数字が高いほど（プラスに向かうほど）酒は辛口になる。そして数字が低いほど（マイナスに向かうほど）甘口になる。「高いほど辛口」と覚えておけばいい。ただし、ゼロは甘口と辛口の中間を意味するのではなく、純水とまったく同じ比重であることを示しているので注意してほしい。最近の日本酒度の標準は、+4くらいである。

だが、この数字は**極端な表示**でないかぎり、それほど役に立たない。甘さと辛さの感覚には、非常に多くのことが影響しているからだ。

comparatively minuscule number of carbonated products exist. While it can be enjoyable, it is quite a different animal from regular sake.

The *Nihonshu-do*

Sometimes called the "Sake Meter Value" in English, the *nihonshu-do* refers to the specific gravity of the sake, i.e., the density of the sake compared to the density of water. More practically, it is a number typically between -3 and +12 that indicates the sweetness or dryness of a sake. **It is entirely unrelated to grade and quality**.

Theoretically, the higher (more positive) the number, the drier the sake. The lower (more negative) the number, the sweeter the sake. Just remember, "Higher is dryer." Note that zero is not neutral in terms of sweet or dry, but rather indicates the exact same density as pure water. The average *nihonshu-do* these days is about +4 or so.

However, this number is not all that useful **except in its extreme manifestations**, since so many things affect the perception of sweet and dry.

🍶 古酒

ほとんどの日本酒は**熟成されることなく、新鮮なうちに消費される**。お酒は集めて貯蔵したりせずに、買ったらすぐに飲むべきである。1年も経てば、味も香りも著しく変化しだすからだ。

とはいえ、熟成させる酒もあって、これもなかなか面白い。ただしワインとは違い、さまざまな方法で熟成することで、さまざまな結果を生むような酒はほとんどない。熟成した酒は、同じ酒の新しいものと比べて決しておいしいとはいえない。数ヵ月熟成させるとおいしくなることも多いが、ほとんどの場合、お酒は出来たての新鮮なうちに飲むことになっている。ただ、おいしい例外も2、3あることは覚えておこう。

🍶 温度

「吟醸」のような高級酒は、たいてい少し冷やして飲むのがいい。もちろん、当然ながら例外もある。それどころか、最近日本では、**ちょっとした燗ブームの復活**が起こっている。そこで、お酒——特に「吟醸」——は少し冷やして（白ワインくらいの温度で）味わってほしいが、ほんのり温めると、とてもおいしい酒もあることを知っておこう。

Aging Sake

Almost all sake **is not aged but is consumed young**. One should not collect or store sake, but rather drink it soon after purchase. Sake will begin to noticeably change in flavor and aroma after about a year.

Some sake is aged, however, and can be interesting. But unlike wine, what little sake is aged is aged in varying ways with varying results. Aged sake is definitely not better than its youthful counterpart. Sake usually benefits from a few months of maturation, but it is almost always meant to be consumed young and fresh. Just remember that there are a few tasty exceptions.

Temperature

Most premium sake like *ginjo* should be consumed slightly chilled. There are of course the requisite exceptions. In fact, there is **a bit of a warmed-sake renaissance** going on in Japan now. So enjoy your sake—and your *ginjo* in particular—slightly chilled (about white wine temperature), but know that some are very enjoyable gently warmed.

🍶 お酒を飲むときの器とガラス製品

ワイングラスがとくに香り高い「吟醸」によく合うが、足つきグラスは日本では滅多に使われない。いっぽう、ワイングラスほど味を引き立てたり、香りを高めることができなくても、伝統的な日本の陶器は、酒を飲むときに手ざわりを楽しみ、見て楽しむという大きな魅力を加えてくれる。そして最も大切なことは、だれが何と言おうと、完璧な形のグラスは1つもないということだ。

🍶 貯蔵

お酒の貯蔵法は簡単である。ワインと同じように扱えばいい。言いかえれば、涼しく、強い光の当たらないところに置くとよい。「生酒」(低温殺菌されていない酒)以外は、冷蔵する必要はない。だが温度が低いほど熟成のスピードが落ち、お酒の風味が損なわれないので、もし冷蔵庫に空きがあるなら、そこに入れよう！

いったん栓を開けたら、一番いいのはワインのように扱って早めに飲むことだ(これは、たいてい問題ない)。お酒の中にはほかより長持ちするものがあるし、**一般に日本酒はワインより扱いが易しい**。経験から言えば、開けてから一週間くらいは大丈夫である。

Vessels and Glassware for Enjoying Sake

Wine glasses work fine, especially for aromatic *ginjo*, although stemware is rarely used in Japan. However, even if it does not flatter flavors and enhance aromas as well, traditional Japanese pottery **adds a very enjoyable tactile and visual appeal** to sake drinking. And, most importantly, there is no one perfect shape of glass, no matter what anyone tells you.

Storage

Storing sake is simple: treat it like a wine. In other words, keep it cool and out of strong light. It does not need to be refrigerated unless it is *namazake* (unpasteurized sake). Since colder temperatures will slow down aging and not hurt the sake at all, if you have room in the refrigerator, keep it there!

Once a bottle is open, the safest thing is to treat it like a bottle of wine and drink it soon (which is not usually a problem). Some sake lasts longer than others, and generally **sake is more forgiving than wine**. As a rule of thumb, after opening you have about a week.

お酒と料理

お酒と料理の組み合わせは、ワインと料理の組み合わせと同じ原則に従う。料理と酒双方の**特徴を補い、高めあうものを探そう**。決まった法則などない！ 決して日本食に限らないし、アジア料理でさえなくていい。うまく合わないこともももちろんあるが、洋食には日本酒にぴったり合う幅広い種類の料理がある。

たしかに、香りが強い料理や、スパイスを多く使った料理は日本酒に合わない。**日本酒の繊細な特徴をかき消してしまうからだ**。明らかに合わないものは除いたうえで、あらゆる魚料理、野菜料理、さらには軽く火を通した肉料理も試してほしい。お酒の用途の広さに、うれしい驚きをおぼえることだろう。

Sake and Food

Sake and food pairing follows the same principles as wine and food pairings: look for things that **complement and enhance aspects of both** the food and the sake. There are no rules! By no means should sake be limited to Japanese food, or even to Asian food. While mismatches are certainly possible, there is a very wide range of Western food with which sake dovetails wonderfully.

Surely, very strongly flavored and spicy dishes are mismatches, **as the subtle aspects of sake will be drowned out**. After removing obviously incongruous pairings from the equation experiment with all forms of fish, vegetables, and even lightly prepared meats. You will be pleasantly surprised at how versatile sake can be.

Part 2 Sake Secrets

日本酒の秘密

1. 「純米」と「純米」でない酒

「純米」の等級と、「純米」でない等級を比べるとどちらがいいか――つまり、米、水、「麹」だけで造られた酒と、この３つの原料に少量の蒸留アルコールを加えて造った酒では、どちらが上か――これは、お酒の世界では興味深い話題だ。**人々の意見は、控えめに言っても多種多様である。**

なかには、「純米」タイプでない酒を、まるで目の敵にしているような団体もある。これにはいくつか理由があるが、どれもまったく根拠のないもので、そのうち２、３は誤りでさえある。米のみを使った「純米」製法だけが、本物の酒造りの方法であり、アルコールを加えるのはイカサマに近いと主張する人々がいる。また、加えたアルコールの味には我慢ならないし、そのせいで二日酔いになると主張する人々もいる。このように中傷する人たちは、「純米」でない酒が、「純米」酒より実際においしいこともあると認めることなど、考えようともしないのだ！

今日製造されている日本酒を全体に見渡してみると、65％あまりが「普通酒」、つまり普段用の「食中酒」である。この最下級の酒の製造過程では、まったく経済的な理由で、**かなりの量のアルコールがたしかに加**

1. *Junmai* vs. Non-*Junmai*

How *junmai* grades compare to non-*junmai* grades—how sake made with only rice, water, and *koji* compares to sake made with these three ingredients plus a bit of pure distilled alcohol—is a topic of interest in the sake world. **Opinions are varied, to say the least**.

In some circles there almost seems to be a vendetta against anything that is not of the *junmai* style. There are a handful of reasons why this is so, although none seems totally valid, and a couple are not even correct. Some folks insist the rice-only *junmai* method is the only true, real way to make sake, or that to add alcohol is almost cheating. Others insist they cannot stand the taste of the added alcohol, or that it gives them a hangover. Such detractors do not even consider acknowledging the ways in which non-*junmai* sake can actually be better than *junmai*!

When we look at all sake produced today, just over 65 percent is *futsu-shu*, or regular "table sake." During the production of this lowest grade of sake, **good dollops of alcohol** are indeed added, and for

えられている。醸造業者はアルコールを加えることによって、**水増しするとまでは言わないまでも**、生産量を著しく増やすことができるし、世間の多くの消費者たちも、そういう酒に十分満足している。実際、この等級の酒は申し分なくおいしい。たしかに「高級」ではないが、それでも楽しめる味なのだ。

　高級酒の範囲——上から35パーセントを占める——に話を進めると、頭に「純米」という言葉がついていない酒はどれでも、少量のアルコールを加えて造られている。「普通酒」でも、加えることができるアルコールの量に制限があるが、高級酒のクラスではさらに厳しい制限がある。

　しかし、ここで本当に重要なのは次のことだ。高級酒になる予定の酒に、アルコールが製造工程で加えられる場合、それは経済的理由によるものではない。理にかなった技術的な理由によるものである。

　いったいどんな理由で？　と、お尋ねになるかもしれない。

　それは、まず第一に、香りと味のためである。味と香りの混合物のなかには、アルコールに溶けるものがある。発酵中の醪が発酵を終えてすぐ、酒と粕を濾し分ける前に、少量のアルコールを加えると、味と香りが米から引き出されて酒の中に溶け込みやすくなる。圧搾の直前に一時的にアルコール量を増やすことで、少なくとも酒の香りが高くなるのだ。また、**貯蔵寿命と安定性**も増してくれる。

purely economic reasons. By adding alcohol brewers can significantly improve **if not stretch yields**, and for many consumers on the street, sake like that is good enough. And in truth, most of that grade of sake is perfectly enjoyable. Certainly not *premium,* but enjoyable nonetheless.

Moving into the realm of premium sake—the top 35 percent—anything that does not have the word *junmai* as a prefix is also made with a bit of added alcohol. While there are limits to how much can be added even to *futsu-shu*, it is limited further in the premium sake classes.

But here is what is really significant: when alcohol is added during production to what will become premium sake, it is not done for economic reasons. It is done for sound, technical reasons.

Like what? you might ask.

Well, **for starters, aroma and flavor**. Some flavor and aroma compounds are soluble in alcohol. If a bit of alcohol is added to the fermenting mash just after fermentation is complete but before the sake is separated from the lees, it becomes easier to draw those flavors and aromas out of the rice and get them into the sake. The temporary increase of alcohol just before pressing helps sake become more aromatic at the least. **It also adds to shelf life and stability**.

日本語には「アル添」という言葉があるが、これは「アルコール添加」の略語である。業界用語であり、公式な言葉ではなく、ラベルにも載っていない。だが「純米」でない酒をひとまとめにして指すには、この方が便利なので、ここでは「アル添」という言葉を使うことにしよう。

　統計によると、純米タイプ（つまり、「純米酒」、「純米吟醸酒」、「純米大吟醸酒」）の消費は合計して、わずかではあるが明らかに増加している。純米派の人が好んで指摘したがるところだ。しかし本当に起こっているのは、「普通酒」と「本醸造酒」の消費が落ちていることだ——それはこれらの酒が「アル添」だからではなく、**低い等級の酒を飲む人が減っているからである**。市場の底辺が収縮しており、しかもその底辺がとても大きいので（すべて「アル添」である）、認識がゆがめられるのだ。

　じつは統計をもっとよく見ると、最高級品の生産がすべて、「吟醸」や「大吟醸」の「アル添」ものを含めて、ゆっくりとだが確実に増えている。つまり、「純米」志向にもかかわらず、**「アル添」の消費はしぼんでいない**。ただ、高級酒が安い酒よりも選ばれるようになってきたということだ。

　「純米」についてのもうひとつの根拠のない説は、これが本来の正しい酒造りの方法で、アルコール添加は **1940 年代の戦時中の米不足**や、それに関連するほかの理由から始まっただけだというものだ。実際には、数世紀前まで遡ると、発酵の弱い酒樽をテコ入れする

There is a word in Japanese, *aru-ten,* which is an abbreviation for *arukoru tenka*, or "added alcohol." It is an industry term, not an official one, and it is not found on labels. But it is a less unwieldy way to refer to all non-*junmai* sake collectively, so let us use it here.

Statistics clearly show that consumption of *junmai* types collectively (i.e., *junmai-shu*, *junmai ginjo*, and *junmai daiginjo*) is growing, albeit minutely. *Junmai* fans love to point this out. But what is really happening is that both *futsu-shu* and *honjozo* consumption are dropping—not because they are *aru-ten*, but rather because **fewer people are drinking lower grades of sake**. The bottom of the market is contracting, but the bottom is so large (and consists of all *aru-ten*!) that it skews perception.

In truth, a closer look at statistics will show that production of all the top grades, including the *aru-ten* versions of *ginjo* and *daiginjo*, is growing slowly but surely. The point is that ***aru-ten* is not contracting** in the face of preferences for *junmai*, but rather that premium sake is being chosen over cheap sake.

Another myth about *junmai* is that it was the original and proper method of making sake, and that adding alcohol only came about **in the 1940s due to wartime rice shortages** and other related reasons. In fact, as far back as several centuries some brewers

ために、時々蒸留アルコールを加える杜氏もいた。だから、この技術は新しいものでも、非伝統的でもないのだ。まさに、日本における酒醸造の驚くべき技であり、名人芸のひとつなのだ。

　元来、「吟醸」酒はすべて「アル添」だった。「吟醸」の醸造法が発達してきた頃、**最後のアルコール添加は不可欠な行程であった**。味と香りをそこまで引き出そうとすると、この工程は絶対に必要だと考えられていたのだ。「吟醸」と「大吟醸」の「純米」ものは、20世紀の終わり頃になってできたものである。

　また、匂いや味で違いがわかると主張する人もいる。だれもが認めるように、安い酒ならこれは簡単である。全体の成分のバランスが薄っぺらく、旨味に欠けていて、甘味のバランスが悪いからだ。だが「吟醸」レベルになると、**この主張は説得力を失う**。完成品のアルコール含有量は「アル添」でないものと同じである。加えられるものは厳しく制限されているし、成分はまったく同じもの、つまりエチルアルコールだからだ。

　さらに大きな誤解は、「アル添」の酒は強化酒だというものだ。たしかに、ほんの一時だけ強化されるが、出荷前に水で薄められて同じ16％前後に下げられる。もちろんこの点には議論の余地があるが、飲むときに強化されていなければ強化酒ではないと、わたしは思う。

would from time to time add distilled alcohol to bolster a weakly fermenting tank of sake. So the technique is neither new nor non-traditional. It is very much a part of the incredible skill and masterful techniques of the craft of brewing sake in Japan.

Originally, all *ginjo* sake was *aru-ten*. When *ginjo* brewing methods were being developed, **adding alcohol at the end was an integral step**. If one was going to go to that extent to bring out flavor and aroma, that step was considered indispensable. The *junmai* versions of *ginjo* and *daiginjo* came later in the 20th century.

Then there are those who insist they can smell and taste the difference. Admittedly, in cheap sake this is easy, as the overall component balance is thin, lacking umami, or is unbalanced in sweetness. But in the realm of the *ginjo* levels, **this is not a valid argument**. The final alcohol content is the same as non-*aru-ten*, what was added was strictly limited, and it is all the same thing: ethyl alcohol.

An even greater misconception is that *aru-ten* sake is fortified. Sure, for a short period of time it was fortified, but it was watered back down to the same 16 percent or so before being shipped. Certainly this point is debatable, but it seems to me that if it is not fortified when we enjoy it, it is not a fortified drink.

かなり大ざっぱな見積もりだが、「アル添」は、同種の「純米」より平均して15パーセント安い。言いかえれば、ふたつの酒が同じ精米歩合の同じ米から造られているのに、「アル添」は約15％も安い。しかも「アル添」という工程のおかげで、かえっていきいきとして、おいしくなる。この点もたしかに議論の余地があるが、わたしはそう思う。だから、「アル添」はコストパフォーマンスの点でも勝っているのだ。

　最後に、日本における日本酒市場の90％が「アル添」酒である。そして、その多くが本当に抜群の酒なのだ！　市場に出ている大半の酒を**即座に**「**批判**」**する**のは妥当ではないだろう。市場の大半を占めているなら、明らかに確かなものだからだ。

　問題全体を違う角度から見てみると、1990年代の中頃から、多くの杜氏たちが、この２つのタイプの可能性を最大限に引き出そうとしているようである。言いかえれば、「純米」タイプには、**こくがあり、少し酸味が強く、豊かな味**になる可能性がある。とくに同種の「アル添」酒に比べて、この方向に進む「純米」酒が増えている。一方「アル添」酒は、より**香り高く、軽やかな味**になる傾向がある。たしかに、どちらにも例外はたくさんあるが、いわば「純米」タイプはより「純米」風に、そして「アル添」タイプはアルコール添加の効果を最大に引き出そうとする杜氏が増えているようだ。

　現在、「純米」だけを製造している「蔵」は25から

A very rough estimation shows that on average, *aru-ten* is about 15 percent cheaper than a corresponding *junmai*. In other words, if two sake are made from the same rice milled to the same degree, the *aru-ten* will be about 15 percent cheaper, but often, thanks to the *aru-ten* process, it will be just as lively and enjoyable. Certainly this point, too, is debatable, but that is how it seems to me. So *aru-ten* wins the cost-performance competition as well.

Finally, 90 percent of the sake market in Japan is *aru-ten* sake. And a lot of it is truly outstanding sake! It **seems inappropriate to summarily "diss"** most of what is out there, since it is obviously valid if it makes up most of the market.

Looking at the whole question from a different angle, since the mid-1990s many brewers seem to be maximizing the potential of the two styles. In other words, *junmai* types have the potential to be **richer, a bit higher in acidity, and fuller**. More and more *junmai* sake are heading in that direction, particularly in comparison to their *aru-ten* counterparts, which tend to be **more aromatic and lighter**. Sure, there are tons of exceptions either way, but it seems that more brewers try to make *junmai* types more *junmai*-esque, so to speak, and to maximize what adding alcohol can do.

Currently, there are twenty-five to thirty *kura* that

30 ある。(日本では日本酒の醸造業者は「酒蔵」と呼ばれ、しばしば「蔵」と省略される)。この数は増加しているが、現存している 1200 の「蔵」の中ではごくわずかである。流行と呼ぶにはとても十分とは言えない。

最後に、「純米」純粋主義者になるのは少しも構わない。純粋主義者になるのは人々の自由だし、どの消費者にもたしかにその権利がある。それもまた楽しいものだ。ただしその道を行くなら、とても多くのよい酒に出会えなくなることは覚悟してほしい。

わたしは個人的には、「純米」反対派ではない。それどころか、たしかに「アル添」タイプより「純米」タイプをよく飲むほうだ。そのかわり、**誤った情報によるインチキ話は避ける**ようにしている。「純米」、「純米吟醸」、「純米大吟醸」はいずれも、同種の「アル添」酒より必ずしもおいしいとは言えないのだ。

make only *junmai*. (A sake brewer in Japan is called a *sakagura*, often shortened to just *kura*.) While this number is increasing, it is still **a drop in the bucket** of the 1,200 that currently exist. That is not quite enough to call it a trend.

In the end, being a *junmai* purist is fine. People are free to be purists; it is certainly the right of any consumer. There is joy in that. But know that should you go that route, you are cutting yourself off from a *lot* of good stuff.

I am personally not anti-*junmai*. In fact, I surely drink more *junmai* types than *aru-ten* types. I am, instead, for **avoiding hype from misinformation**. As good as *junmai*, *junmai ginjo*, and *junmai daiginjo* are, they are not *unequivocally* better than their *aru-ten* counterparts.

2. 生酒

「生酒」、つまり低温殺菌されていない日本酒のことも、もうひとつの話題として説明しておいたほうがいいだろう。「生」は、時には低温殺菌された酒より**若々しく、新鮮で、活力があり、いきいきした味わい**になることがある。もちろん変質しやすいので、悪くならないようしっかり冷蔵しておかなければならない。しかし、「生酒」（この複合語では、「サケ」の「サ」は「ザ」と発音する）という種類全体としては、低温殺菌した同種の酒より必ずしもおいしいとは限らない。

市場にあるほとんどの酒は、**熱を加えることによって殺菌されている**。これは、酒の品質を安定させるために行われる。空気中には細菌がおり、もし酒の中に入ると、「麹」に残っている酵素活動の副産物を食べて増殖するからだ。熱によって「麹」は活性を失い、細菌も死滅する。ただし、低温にすると有害な活動が抑えられるので、低温殺菌していない酒でも、冷蔵保存すればあまりダメージを受けずにすむ。

昔は、「生酒」は希少であった。その理由のひとつには、酒を販売した相手が全員正しく取り扱ってくれるかどうか、生産者には保証できないということがあ

2. *Namazake*

Namazake, i.e., sake that has not been pasteurized, is another topic that could benefit from some clarification. *Nama* can sometimes be more **youthful, fresh, zippy, and lively** than sake that has been pasteurized. It is of course much less stable and must be kept quite cold to ensure it does not go bad. However, *namazake* (the *s* of "sake" becomes a *z* in this compound) as a category is *not* indisputably better than its pasteurized counterpart.

Almost all sake on the market **has been pasteurized by heating it**. This is done to stabilize sake, as there are bacteria in the air that can, if present, feed on by-products of enzymatic activity remaining from the *koji*. Heat deactivates the *koji* and exterminates the bacteria. Since cold temperatures restrain that detrimental activity, a sake that has not been pasteurized will be spared undue damage if kept refrigerated.

In the past, *namazake* was rare, in part because producers could not guarantee that everyone to whom their sake was distributed would handle it

る。ずっと前は、「生酒」は「蔵」でしか飲めなかったものだ。今日でも、日本酒市場全体のごく一部でしかない。おそらく、そのために**希少で特別という感じ**があり、多くの人々を惹きつけるのだろう。だが、低温殺菌された酒のほうが**魅力が少ない**ということはない。まったく別のもの、それだけのことだ。実際、この2つのタイプはまるで違っている。たとえば、1つの樽の酒の半分を低温殺菌し、もう半分を「生」のままにしたら、その直後も、のちの熟成の段階でも、2つの味と香りは永久に違ったものになる——この一対の酒は**決して一致することはない**のだ。しかし、どちらがおいしいということはない。

　「生」には、すぐに訴えかけてくる魅力があるのは事実だ。「生」によくある（ただし、いつもあるわけではない！）新鮮でいきいきした香りは、人を惹きつけ、すぐに良い反応を引き起こす。しかし、**これ見よがしでもあるその特徴**が、ほとんどの「生」に共通しており、じつはそれが酒のほのかで深い特徴の邪魔をしてしまうのだ。わたしの意見では、「生」風の特徴が、深みを味わうのを妨げるベールとなることが非常によくあると思う。

　言いかえれば、酒の香りを嗅ぎ、味わい、そして「ああ、『生』だ」と思う。それだけでも人に訴えるものが**まるでないわけではないが**、そうなのだ。これでおしまい。これでは全体像の紹介にならないのはわかっているが、もし低温殺菌されていれば、その酒について

properly. Long ago, one could only drink *namazake* at the *kura*. Even today, it is a very small part of the overall sake market. Perhaps that gives it **a sense of being rare and special,** which many people find appealing. However, pasteurized sake is **not a lesser manifestation**. It's just different; that's all. In fact, the two types are very different. If, for example, half of a given batch of sake were to be pasteurized and the other half left as *nama*, how the two would taste and smell immediately afterward and the paths of maturation they would take would be forever altered—and **never the twain shall meet**. But neither one would be better than the other.

It is true that *nama* has an immediate appeal. The fresh, lively aromatics often (but not always!) found in *nama* can draw one in and evoke an immediate, positive response. However, **that same ostentatious aspect** is something common to almost all *nama* and can actually get in the way of subtler, deeper aspects of the sake. To me, very often the *nama*-esque qualities of a sake create a veil that prevents me from seeing into its depths.

In other words, I smell and taste a sake and think, "It's *nama*." **While that alone is not at all unappealing**, that's it; I'm done. I know right there that I am not being shown the entire picture, that I **would be able to sense more** about the sake if it

もっと多くのことを感じることができただろうにと思う。これは、お酒について語ることがほかにないという意味ではない——まだまだ無数の楽しみがある。複雑な香り、味わい、舌ざわり、量感、酸味……。だが同時に、「生」では感じられない特徴のなかに、繊細さと深みが隠れているのがわかるのだ。それにはたいてい失望させられる。

　誇張を避けるために、すべての「生酒」が、覆いとなるベールを作るわけではないことを指摘しておきたい。微妙な深みと、おもしろい複雑さを見せる「生酒」もたしかにある。問題はそういう品質を、時間や、温度、酸素の影響を受けないよう維持するのが非常に難しいということだ。そういう酒もいいかもしれないが、必ずしも優れているとはいえない。それなりにおいしいというだけである。わたしに言わせれば、「生酒」は得るものが少なく、リスクが大きい。

　なぜこの点についてくどくどと論じるのか？ それは、流通網のだれもが——生産者から販売業者、そしてレストランや小売店の店員まで——「生」を特別なものとしてしつこくすすめ、このほうがおいしいと絶賛するのを、しょっちゅう目にするからである。たしかに製品を売り込むのは大切なことだ（我々消費者も特別で珍しいものが好きである）。だがこういう誤った情報は、長い目で見ると、お酒の理解と評価に悪影響を及ぼしかねない。

　もちろん意見はさまざまだし、お酒の何を保つのが大事か、いろいろな考え方がある。たとえば、もし醸

had been pasteurized. This does not mean I can tell nothing else about a sake—there are still countless things to enjoy: aromatic compounds, flavors, textures, volume, acidity.... However, at the same time I realize subtlety and depth are among those aspects to which I will not be treated if the sake is *nama*. And that, often, is disappointing.

To avoid exaggeration, let me point out that not all *namazake* present the obscuring veil. There are certainly *namazake* that exhibit nuanced depth and enjoyable complexity. The issue is that such qualities are very hard to maintain against the enemies of time, temperature, and oxygen. As good as such sake may be, it is not overtly superior; it is just good for what it is. To me, with *namazake* there is little to be gained and much at risk.

Why do I belabor this point? Because all too often I see everyone in the distribution chain—from producers to distributor sales staff and even restaurants and retailers—touting *nama* as special or hailing it as better. Surely, while marketing their products is important (and we consumers love the special and rare), this kind of misinformation can adversely affect long-term understanding and appreciation of sake.

Of course, opinions vary, and there are different ideas about what is important to maintain in a sake. If,

造されたときの状態にできるだけ近い酒が好みならば、なんといっても「生」が理想的だろう。**偏った嗜好がある**というリスクは避けられないものだが、それでもなお、お酒を評価するひとつの妥当な方法ではある。

　低温殺菌や、それを省く際の技術的な点について、さらに2、3話しておくのもいいだろう。ほとんどの酒は実際は2回殺菌される。1回目は醸造が完成した後、そして2回目は貯蔵タンクから瓶詰めされるときだ。酒が空気にさらされるたびに、やっかいな細菌が忍び込みかねない。加熱することで、ダメージを受ける機会を最小限に減らせるのだ。

　だがよく気をつければ、品質の安定性を損なうことなく、2回の殺菌のうち1回を省くことができる。酒を貯蔵するまえに1度低温殺菌し、瓶詰めするまで周囲の空気に触れないようにすれば、2回目の低温殺菌は不要である。あるいは、熟成貯蔵までと熟成中の間、十分に冷やしておいて、瓶詰めする際に適切に低温殺菌するならば、2回のうち1回目の殺菌は省いてもかまわない。

　最初の低温殺菌を省く場合、製品は「生貯蔵」(「生」で貯蔵されたもの)と呼ばれ、2回目を省く場合、「生詰め」(「生」で瓶詰めされたもの)と呼ばれる。後者で秋にだけ見られる季節ものを「冷やおろし」と呼ぶが、技術的には同じものである。

for example, you prefer sake that is as close as possible to what it was when it was brewed, by all means *nama* will approach that ideal. There are inherent risks, **as there are with any predilection**, but it is nonetheless a valid way to assess sake.

A few more technical points about pasteurization or the lack thereof will be useful. Most sake is actually pasteurized twice: once after brewing is completed, and a second time when it moves from storage tanks to bottles. Any time the sake is exposed to the air there is a chance that offending bacteria might sneak their way in. Heating it will minimize the chances of damage.

However, if care is taken, one of the two can be skipped without sacrificing stability. If a sake is pasteurized once before storage and protected from the ambient air on its way to the bottle, the second of the two pasteurizations is not necessary. Alternatively, if it is kept cold enough on the way to and during maturation storage but is properly pasteurized on the way to the bottle, the first of the two can be eliminated.

When the first pasteurization is skipped, the product is called *nama-chozo* (stored *nama*), and if the second one is omitted it is called *nama-tsume* (bottled *nama*). A seasonal variation on the latter seen only in the fall is *hiya-oroshi*, but technically it is

こういう変わり種は受けねらいのように見えるかもしれないが、その目的は、出来たての酒の新鮮さを維持しながら、安定した品質も提供しようとするものだ。**さきほどは痛烈に非難したけれども、低温殺菌は少ないほどいい。**昔は、といってもおそらく1980年代までだが、**酒を劣化させないことが何よりも優先されていた。**劣化すると、文字どおり収入がフイになってしまうからだ。その頃は、低温殺菌はとても疲れる大変な作業だった。しかし技術的な理解が向上したため、杜氏たちは無数の新しい方法を使って低温殺菌することを学んだ。非常にすばやい熱交換器や、詰めたばかりの瓶に温水と冷水をかけたりというような方法だ。どの方法が最善かについては無数の意見があるが、今日、技術はさらに進んで、酒造りを支えるものとなっている。

低温殺菌していない酒を表すのに、「生酒」という言葉のかわりに、「生生」や「本生」という言葉が時々使われる。これは、その酒が1度も低温殺菌されていないこと、また、杜氏が低温殺菌することなど「考え」もしなかったことを強調するためである。だがこの3つの言葉——「生酒」、「生生」、そして「本生」——は、すべて同じものを指している。

もうひとつ、事実に近いので覚えておくといいのは、「生」だからといって、冷蔵保存しないと絶対に劣化するわけではないということだ。製造した「蔵」が十分に清潔なら、細菌がはじめから入っていないとい

the same.

While these variants may seem gimmicky, the goal is to maintain some sense of the sake's youth but also provide stability. **My diatribe notwithstanding**, the less pasteurization the better. In the old days, which ended perhaps in the 1980s, **the priority was to ensure the sake did not go bad**, as that would be literally revenue down the drain. Back then, pasteurization was a much more punishing process. But as technical understanding has progressed, brewers have learned to pasteurize using a myriad of new ways, like lightning-quick heat exchangers, or hot-then-cold showers over just-filled bottles. There are countless opinions about which methods are best, but techniques are much more advanced and supportive of the sake these days.

Instead of the term *namazake* to refer to unpasteurized sake, the term *nama-nama* or *hon-nama* is sometimes used to emphasize that the sake was not pasteurized even once, that the brewer didn't even *think* about pasteurizing it. But these three terms—*namazake*, *nama-nama*, and *hon-nama*—all mean the same thing.

Another factoid worth remembering is that just because a sake is *nama* does not guarantee it will go bad if not refrigerated. If the *kura* in which it was produced is clean enough, there is a good chance that

う幸運もある。ただし、「生酒」は冷蔵保存しないと**駄目になる可能性がきわめて高い**。

では、どれくらい冷やせばいいのか？ **最適な温度は絶対にこれだと決まっているわけではないが**、一般に冷たいほどいい。摂氏5度（華氏41度）なら、まず間違いなく安心であり、それより2、3度高くてもそれほど品質を損ねることはない。「十分冷やして」となると、なかなか厄介なものである。だが1、2時間冷蔵庫から出しても影響はないし、日本から帰る飛行機でかかる時間くらいは問題ない。1日や、2日でも大丈夫。ただしそのあとは、さまざまな原則や、早く冷たい場所に戻すことに注意を払うようにしよう。

「生酒」は冷蔵しないと「劣化」しやすいが、**どの程度変質したら劣化なのかは、はっきりしない問題だ**。はじめは、とくに酸素が入ると「生酒」は変質して、むしろおいしさの特徴がはっきりと表れる。際立つ香りは、不快ではないものの、木のような鼻につく香りである。この段階ではまだ十分飲むことができるが、このタイプの香りは、酒のほのかな特徴を覆い隠すベールになってしまう。「生酒」がさらに変質すると、このベールは厚くなってカーテンになり、やがて紛れもない壁になる。もしそのまま変質が進みすぎると、酒は見た目に濁り、イーストかチーズのような匂いがしてくる。この状態を「火落ち」といい、いくら大目に見ても、その酒はもう飲めない。

bacteria never entered the sake in the first place. But the potential for *namazake* to **go south** is significantly higher if it is not kept refrigerated

Just how cold is cold enough? **There is no one absolute temperature that is best**, but in general, colder is better. Arguably, 5°C (41°F) is safe, and a few degrees higher would not be disastrous. "Cold enough" is a matter of one's threshold for trouble. An hour or two out of the refrigerator will not affect anything, nor will the time spent on a plane ride home from Japan. Nor will a day, or even two. But after that, it is time to heed the principles involved and time to get it back to a cold environment.

Namazake can "go bad" if not kept cold, but **just how bad is bad is not a black-and-white issue**. At first, especially if oxygen is involved, *namazake* will head south by exhibiting more of what makes it enjoyable: prominent aromas that, while not unpleasant, can be woody and cloying. At this stage it is still perfectly drinkable, but these types of aromas constitute the veil covering the subtler aspects of the sake. As *namazake* gets worse, the veil thickens to a curtain and then a veritable wall. If things are permitted to progress too much, the sake will become cloudy in appearance and yeasty and cheesy in aromas. This condition is called *hiochi,* and the sake is undrinkable, to say the least.

劣化した「生酒」の濁りは、ふつうの「にごり酒」の濁りとは別のものである。「にごり」では、沈殿物は落ち着いているが、劣化した「生」では沈殿物が全体に浮遊しており、糸のように連なって見えることが多い。それを目印にして避けるといいだろう。

　はっきりさせておくが、わたしは「生」反対派ではない。全然違う！　どちらかといえば、解説のプロである。最終的な分析としては、どの酒も──「生」も低温殺菌された酒も──人によって好みに合う。「生酒」はすばらしい酒のこともある。だだ、低温殺菌された酒よりおいしいということはない。少なくとも、「生」であるというだけで単純においしいとは言えないのだ。

The cloudiness in *namazake* gone bad is different from that of regular *nigorizake*. In *nigori*, the sediment will settle, whereas in bad *nama* it will float suspended throughout, often in visible strands. That would be your cue to avoid it.

For the record, I am not anti-*nama*. Not at all! I am, if anything, pro-clarification. In the final analysis, any sake—*nama* or pasteurized—is in the palate of the beholder. *Namazake* can be wonderful. But it is not better than pasteurized sake, at least not simply by virtue of just being *nama*.

3. 古酒

　お酒は出来たてのうちに飲むほうがいい。収集して貯蔵したり、熟成させようとする人はいないだろう。一般に、**購入したら早く飲むほうがいいのだ**。

　「しかし例外はある」。お酒の世界にはいつも必ず例外がある。

　もちろん、上述したのは伝統的な論理である。たいていの場合、お酒は出来たてで新鮮なうちに飲むのがベストだ。たしかに、市場に出す前に2年以上製品を熟成させる酒蔵もある。だが消費者の手に届いたら、なるべく早く飲むように、また、それ以上熟成させないようにと、彼らも望んでいる。

　しかし、古酒もたしかに存在する。3年、5年、10年もの、ときにはもっと古い製品がある。古酒は、とても興味深いものでもあるのだ。しかし市場では非常に少ない。ほとんどの酒蔵は古酒を造らない。**非常にニッチな特殊市場**であり、これからもずっとそうだろう。だが魅力的な味になる可能性は大きいので、よく理解しておく価値は十分にある。

　古酒の話を切り出すことに、わたしはいつも、ため

3. Aged Sake

Sake should be consumed while still young; you do not want to collect it, lay it down, or age it. Generally, **the sooner after purchasing you drink it, the better**.

But there are exceptions. There are *always* exceptions in the sake world.

In truth, the above is the conventional logic. Almost always, sake is best enjoyed young and fresh. Certainly some brewers will mature their product before shipping it to the market, often upward of two years. But once it gets to you, they expect you to enjoy it relatively soon, and not age it any longer.

However, aged sake does exist. There are products out there that are three-, five-, and ten-year-aged sake, and occasionally even older. Aged sake can be very, very interesting. But it is an extremely small part of the market. Most brewers do not make any aged sake at all. It is **very much a niche sector** and will likely always remain so. But because it holds great potential for engaging enjoyment, it is well worth understanding thoroughly.

I am usually quite reticent to broach the topic

らいを覚えてしまう。高価だし、見つけにくいし、ふつうの酒とはまったく別の代物だし、ことを始めるのによい方法とは決して言えない──まったく別物なのだ。熟成のやり方には、さまざまに入り組んだ多くの方法があるので、理解するのは難しい。どうやって古酒になるかさえ、いろいろありすぎて簡潔に伝えることができない。たぶん、わたしが古酒の奨励に慎重になる最大の理由は、**人はときに、珍しくて高価で、特別なものを手に入れたがるからなのだ**。古酒は希少なので、ここに問題が起こってしまう。珍しさや、見た目の価値や、さらには値段のせいで気に入った人々は、飲んでみてがっかりしたときに、背中を向けてほかの高級な飲み物へ向かってしまうかもしれない──どうかそんなことになりませんように！　正統なお酒の世界を後回しにせずに、しっかり「経験」しながら、だんだんと古酒をたしなむようになってほしい。

とはいえ、古酒を積極的にすすめる気はないものの、わたしは古酒に魅了されているし、とてもよく飲んでいる。**日本酒通になりたいなら、いつかは古酒について学ぶ必要があるだろう**。

古酒は以前からあったが──記録は 13 世紀までさかのぼる──いつの時代でも、ほとんどの人が飲むのは新しい酒で、生産されるのもそうだった。しかも 1800 年代の後半、今日の酒税法のようなものができたとき、酒蔵は醸造した酒の量に課税された。製品が

of aged sake. It is expensive, hard to find, a totally different animal from regular sake, and most definitely not a better way to do things—it's just different. The methodology is a hassle to grasp, as there are many variables involved and different ways to mature. Even just how aged sake turns out is far too varied to convey concisely. Perhaps the biggest reason I am wary to promote aged sake is that **sometimes people like to latch on to the rare, the expensive, and the special**. This presents a problem because so little aged sake exists. If people come to like it because of its rarity, perceived value, or even price, then when they find they can get so little of it, they may leave it behind and move on to—God forbid!—another premium beverage. I would much prefer folks come to know and appreciate aged sake gradually, by going *through* the world of orthodox sake, and not around it.

Still, while I may shy away from actively promoting aged sake, I am fascinated by it and enjoy it immensely. **Should you pursue sake connoisseurship**, aged sake is eventually a must-study.

Although some aged sake has always existed—records of it go back to the 13th century—young sake has always been what most people drank and comprised most of what was produced. But back in the late 1800s, when the modern-day laws governing

売れたかどうかに関わりなく、税金は定期的に徴収された。だから違法ではないものの、すでに税金を払った製品を、売らずに数年待つ気にはとてもなれなかったのだ。酒を熟成させることにも、その結果にもあまり興味がなかった。もし売れなかったら、支払った税金のぶんだけ損をするからだ。そのため、古酒は全般的になくなっていったのである。

1940年代の後半に法律が改正され、酒蔵は醸造したものでなく、販売したものに課税されるようになった。その後しばらくして、一握りの――念のために言うが、ほんの一握りの――酒蔵が古酒の製造を試みるようになった。だが今日でも、**ほとんどの酒蔵は手を出さず、長期間熟成された酒は、全体の1%よりはるかに少ない。**

ことによると、最近の事情のおかげで、**お酒の熟成方法が大きく変わったのかもしれない。**たとえば、冷たい貯蔵室の温度で熟成させることができるし、冷蔵庫ならもっと低い温度にもできる。鋼鉄のタンクで、小さなガラス瓶で、また、いろんな大きさの陶器でさえ熟成できる。2年から20年まで、さまざまな期間で熟成させることも可能だ。どの選択も、お酒にそれぞれの特徴を与えることになる。

また当然のことだが、酒蔵がはじめに使う酒の種

sake were written, sake brewers were taxed on the amount of sake they brewed. Taxes were collected regularly, whether or not the product had been sold. As such, while not illegal, there was very little motivation to wait several years to sell product on which tax had already been paid. Nor was there much interest in aging product and seeing how it turned out, since if it did not sell, the brewer would lose revenue as well as the tax paid. So, by and large, aged sake ceased to exist.

The law changed in the late 1940s, and brewers began to be taxed on what was sold, not what was brewed. Soon after that, a handful—just a handful, mind you—of brewers began to experiment with aging sake. But even today, **most brewers do not mess with it**, and way less than 1 percent of all sake is aged any significant length of time.

Possibly because it is a comparatively recent thing, just **how a sake is aged varies hugely**. For example, sake can be aged at cool cellar temperatures, or at any one of several lower temperatures via refrigeration. It can be aged in steel brewing tanks, small glass bottles, or even ceramic vessels of various sizes. It can be matured for varying lengths of time ranging from two to twenty years. Each one of these choices imparts a different character to the sake.

Also, the type of sake a brewer starts with greatly

類が、結果に大きく影響する。精米歩合の高い米で造る、軽い口当たりの「大吟醸」を熟成させる場合と、アミノ酸が多くてどっしりとした味わいの、こくのある「純米」の場合とでは、まるで違う味になる。精米歩合だけでなく、アルコール添加、もともとの酸味や、糖とアミノ酸の含有量、またほかの要因が酒の熟成に影響する。

想像できると思うが、熟成と原材料の組み合わせは無限にあるので、**古酒の味は、まさに色とりどりである**。たとえば、軽やかで辛口の「大吟醸」を冷蔵温度で５年間、瓶で熟成させると、よりまろやかな味になることがある──つまり、大いに品質が上がるのだ。ほかの極端な例では、精米歩合の低い米でこくのある「純米」を造り、タンクで10年間熟成させる。すると、土臭い、ほとんどカビ臭いような、こくがあって旨味の多い酒になり、おまけにきれいな琥珀色になるのだ。

一般に、酒は熟成させると、色、土臭さ、こくが増し、酸味も際立つようになる。シェリー酒の熟成の仕方と似ていることが多い。だが重要なことは、**醸造と貯蔵の状態によって、結果は大きく変化する**ということだ。

古酒を指す言葉が２、３ある。最もわかりやすいのは「古酒」で、「古い」酒という意味だ。だがこの言葉

affects the outcome, naturally enough. A light *daiginjo* made with highly milled rice will mature much differently from a rich *junmai* with its heavy, amino-acid-laden flavor. Not only the milling rate but the added alcohol, the original acidity, the original sugar and amino acid content, and other factors will affect how a sake matures.

As you can imagine, with the myriad of possible combinations of aging and ingredients, **how aged sake will taste is all over the map**. For example, a light and dry *daiginjo* matured for five years at refrigerated temperatures in the bottle might just end up with a more well-rounded flavor—and be vastly improved by that. The other extreme would see a rich *junmai* made with rice milled much less, and then aged in tanks for ten years. This would surely be earthy, almost musty perhaps, rich and umami-laden, and quite amber in color to boot.

In general, this is what happens to sake: it takes on color, earthiness, and richness, and the acidity can become more prominent as well. Often, sake matures in much the way that a sherry matures. But it is important to remember that **the results will vary greatly depending on the conditions of both brewing and storage**.

There are a couple of terms that refer to aged sake. The simplest is *koshu*, which means "old" sake.

には、放っておかれたもの、つまり不注意で古くなってしまった酒というニュアンスがある。そこで、故意に熟成させた酒を指すために、「長期熟成酒」という言葉のほうがよく使われる。たいそうな言葉を使うほど、たいそうな味だとごまかしているものだが、おそらく、これはただの偶然だろう。

お酒の世界には、何年ものというような、**公式のヴィンテージ制度はない**。これには理由が2つある。ひとつには、ほとんどの酒は熟成されないからだ。製品がないのでは、醸造年度の話などありえない。2つ目には、ほとんどの酒蔵が目指しているのは、**毎年の製品の一貫性**だからだ。継続して変わらないことが目標ならば、ある年がとくによかったと自慢する制度は不要である。ただし、酒のラベルに「ヴィンテージ」という言葉を見かけることがあるが、それは古酒ということを示しているだけで、ヴィンテージ制度が存在するわけではない。

酒蔵が酒を熟成させると、醸造した年を使って、酒の年齢を表すことがよくある。だが、この年はカレンダーの年とは一致しない。

お酒は1年のうちの寒い時期(秋に始まり、翌春に終わる)に醸造されるからで、**醸造時期はカレンダーでは2年にまたがる**。酒蔵はBY、つまり「醸造年度」を付記する。これは、7月1日から翌年の6月30日までの1年間のことだ。たとえば「2013 BY」は、2013年7月1日に始まり、2014年6月30日に終わる。2013年11月に醸造された酒と、2014年4月に醸造された

However, the nuance of this term is such that it can imply something left lying around, i.e., sake that has been inadvertently aged. As such, to refer to sake that has been deliberately matured, the term *chokijukuseishu* is more common. The bigger term belies its bigger flavors, but perhaps that is just a coincidence.

Note that **an official vintage system does not exist** in the sake world. There are two reasons for this. One is that most sake is not aged. A vintage year is hard to speak about when there is no product. Second, the goal of most sake producers is **consistency from year to year for a given product**. There is no need for a system that vaunts the merits of a particular year when the goal is continuity of style. However, one does see the word "vintage" on sake labels sometimes, although it just indicates aged sake rather than any existing vintage system.

When brewers age sake, they often refer to its age by using the year in which it was brewed. This year does not, however, correspond with a calendar year.

Because sake is brewed in the cold part of the year (beginning in autumn and finishing the following spring), **any given brewing season will straddle two calendar years**. Brewers refer to a given BY, or "brewing year," which is a one-year period that begins July 1 and ends June 30 of the following year. As an example, "2013 BY" would begin on July 1,

酒は、どちらも「2013 BY」となる。つまり、同じ BY がラベルに書かれていれば、同じ醸造時期に造られたものということだ。

　複雑に思えるかもしれないが、お酒の醸造の世界では、とても理にかなったやり方なのだ。
　もちろん、**自分で酒を熟成させてみる**こともできる。多くのことを学べるし、結果に満足するかもしれない。だがそれは、醸造業者が意図していた飲みかたでは決してない。熟成させると、まったく別の酒になるからだ。だが酒が熟成するとどうなるか、じかに学ぶために、犠牲にする価値はあるかもしれない。

　海外で日本酒の評価が高まるなか、市場の 99％を占める正統な新酒に焦点をあてるのがベストかもしれない。しかし、**古酒にも計り知れない魅力がある**。新酒よりおいしいのではなく、別のものとして、学ぶ値打ちは十分にあるのだ。

2013, and end on June 30, 2014. A sake brewed in November 2013 and one brewed in April 2014 would both be part of "2013 BY." This ensures that all the sake labeled with a given BY was made in the same brewing season.

As complicated as it might seem here, it makes great sense in the sake-brewing world.

Of course, it is possible to **experiment and age sake yourself**. You would learn a lot and might even like the result. But what you would *not* be doing is enjoying your sake the way the brewer intended you to enjoy it, as it would have become a different sake altogether. But it might be worth that sacrifice to learn firsthand how sake matures.

While it seems best for the burgeoning world of sake appreciation outside Japan that we all focus on the 99 percent of the market that is orthodox young sake, **aged sake has its immense appeal as well**. It's not better than young sake, just different, but well worth the effort to learn about.

4. 日本酒度

「情報過多」というものがある。消費者に役立つようにと、または商品への興味を引こうとして、業界は怪しげで不必要なデータをばらまく。そんなデータは消費者を混乱させるか、もっと悪いことには、しりごみさせてしまうものだ。「日本酒度」はそういう悪者だと、わたしは思う。

「日本酒度」は英語で「サケ・メーター・バリュー」と訳されることが多く、これは直訳でわかりやすい。英語のラベルではよく SMV と略され、**酒の甘さと辛さを示す数字**とされているが、実際にはそうではない。少なくとも、ちゃんと示してはいない。

ほとんどの酒の「日本酒度」は、− 2 から + 10 の間だが、もっと高かったり低かったりもする。「高いほど辛口」と覚えておけばいい。数字が高いほど酒は辛口で、低いほど甘口だ。ただし、おおよその目安である。

サケ・メーター・バリューは、実際は**純水に対する酒の比重**であり、比重計という機器で測定される。ゼロの測定値は、甘口と辛口の「中間」を指すのではなく、比重が水と同じであることを示している。

4. The *Nihonshu-do*

There is such a thing as "too much information." Often, in an attempt to be helpful to consumers, or in an effort to make things seem more interesting, the industry disseminates data of dubious usefulness, which just confuses, or worse, intimidates. I think the *nihonshu-do* is one such culprit.

The *nihonshu-do* is often translated into English as the "Sake Meter Value," a direct translation that works fine. Often abbreviated SMV on English-language labels, it is **a number associated with a sake that is supposed to indicate sweetness or dryness**, but in reality it does not. At least not very well.

The *nihonshu-do* is usually between −2 and +10 for most sake, although it could be much higher or lower. Just remember "higher is dryer": the higher the number, the dryer the sake, and the lower the number, the sweeter the sake. More or less.

Sake Meter Value actually refers to **the density of the sake compared to the density of pure water** and is measured with an instrument called a hydrometer. A measurement of zero does not indicate "neutral" in

ラベルにその数字が書いてある場合、酒に含まれる糖の量を推測できるが、どれくらい甘いか辛いかは、この数字だけでは大してわからない。ここに問題がある。

お酒には、ほかの特徴がいくつかあって、それが甘さと辛さの感覚全般に影響しているのだ。それぞれがある程度の割合で、誤りを指摘してくれることだろう。では、その特徴を2、3見てみよう。

まず、酸味について考えよう。酸味があると、酒は辛く感じやすい。同じ「日本酒度」の2つの酒がある場合、**酸味が強いほうが辛く感じるのだ。**この効果はかなり大きいので、「日本酒度」の解釈は、25％誤っていると言える。

つぎに、温度を見てみよう。温度によって、甘さと辛さの感覚は大きく変わってくる。少なくともある温度までは、**温かいほど甘さを感じやすい人が多い。**酒は冷のときと、室温のとき、燗のときで、甘口か辛口か、まったく違うようになりかねない。このことでも、25％誤っていると言えるだろう。

当然、お酒と一緒に楽しむ料理についても同じことが言える。少し思いきって簡略化すると、塩辛い料理やスナックは酒の甘さを引き立てることだろう。これ

terms of sweet and dry, but rather a density equal to that of water.

Although the number we see on the label, when it's provided, gives us an approximation of the sugar content of the sake, this alone will not tell us much about how sweet or dry the sake tastes. Therein lies the problem.

There are a handful of other aspects of a sake that will affect the overall sensation of sweet and dry, and each one of these will contribute a certain percentage of error. Let's look at a few of these.

First, consider acidity, which can make a sake taste drier. Between two sake with the same *nihonshu-do*, the one with **the higher acidity will taste drier**. This effect can be significant and can induce perhaps a 25 percent error to the *nihonshu-do* reading.

Next let's look at temperature, which can make our perceptions of sweet and dry vary hugely. For many people **sweetness becomes more noticeable at warmer temperatures**, at least to a certain point. A sake might taste entirely different in terms of sweetness and dryness when tasted chilled versus at room temperature or warmer. This might also impart a 25 percent error.

Naturally, the food with which we enjoy a sake will have its say as well. Oversimplifying just a bit, a saltier dish or snack will bring out an apparent

で、さらに25％の誤りを追加しよう。

そしてもちろん、個人の好みがある。ある人が甘いと思っても、隣の人はそう感じないかもしれない。また、いくつかの酒を飲む場合、先に飲んだ酒が、後で飲む酒の味に影響することもある。たとえば生粋の辛口の酒を飲んだ後では、どんな酒でも先と比べて甘く感じるだろう。この2つの要因で、さらに50％の誤りを付け加えよう。

ほぼ間違いなく、香りも影響していると言っていい。たとえばリンゴ、バナナ、メロンのような「吟醸」の香りをかぐと、辛口ではなく甘口だと思いやすい。また、「生」（低温殺菌されていない酒）の場合も、特有の香りのせいで酒が甘いと誤解することがよくある。ここでも、25％の誤りが課されそうだ。

以上の要因を考え、誤っている可能性を加算すると150％になる。これは基本的に、「日本酒度」が常に間違っていることを、そしてそれ以上のことを意味している。

誇張は抜きにして、大切なことは、「日本酒度」だけでは何の正確な数値にもならないし、ましてや甘さや辛さを示すことはできないということだ。だが、まったく無用の数字だと言うのではない。実際的な使い方として、極端な表示がある場合には、「日本酒度」で甘口・辛口がわかると覚えておこう。＋10なら、だれが飲んでも辛口だし、－2なら甘口だ。だがその間の

sweetness in a given sake. Add another 25 percent error on for this.

And, of course, there is personal taste. What one person considers sweet in a sake might not be so for the next person. Also, if you taste several sake, what you tasted just a moment ago can affect what you sense afterward. After a bone-dry sake, for example, anything else will taste sweet by comparison. Tack on another 50 percent error for these two factors.

Arguably, aromatics also affect things. When sensing apple, banana, or melon in the aromas of a *ginjo*, for example, we tend to think sweet rather than dry. And when a sake is *nama* (unpasteurized) the attendant aromas very commonly mislead people into thinking a sake is sweeter. Here again we might see a 25 percent error imposed.

Considering the above factors, we have a combined potential error of 150 percent, which basically means the *nihonshu-do* is wrong all the time, and then some.

Hyperbole aside, the point is that the *nihonshu-do* is by itself not a very accurate measurement of anything, much less sweet or dry. But that is not to say it is a totally useless number. A practical way to use it is to remember that *in its extreme manifestations* the *nihonshu-do* is a measurement of sweet and dry. A +10 will come across as dry to anyone; a −2 will

数字では、「日本酒度」はまるで役に立たない。

じつは、これは**一般の消費者向けのものではない**。上述したように、比重計による測定値なので、ワインやビールを造る際に使用する比重計の数値と数字上は似ている。この数値は醸造工程で使われる技術的な道具であり、デンプンから糖への変化と、糖からアルコールへの変化の進み具合を知るための測定値なのだ。どの酒にも、最終的に目標とする「日本酒度」の数値があるだろう。しかしこれは、酒の性質を決めるさまざまな要因や決断のうちの一面でしかない。

いつのまにか、この情報をラベルに載せる酒蔵が現れはじめ、そのうち過度の重要性を負うようになったのだ。

「日本酒度」をラベルに記載することは**不要だし、規制もない**。高級酒以外の酒のラベルに記載されていることは滅多にないし、高級酒でも半分程度である。世間の目から隠そうとする者はだれもいない（労を惜しまないなら、どの酒もインターネットで調べられる）。しかし、「日本酒度」が消費者にとって有意義な情報だと考えている人は多くない。

わたし自身は積極的に見ないが、ラベルを調べているときに視界に入ってきても、目を覆うようなことはしない。大して重要ではない、それだけのことだ。

seem sweet. But in between those extremities, the *nihonshu-do* is fairly useless.

In truth, it was **never meant for public consumption**. As mentioned above, it is a hydrometer reading and has a mathematical correlation to hydrometer readings used in making wine and beer. It is a technical tool used during the brewing process, a measurement that tells the brewer how both starch-to-sugar and sugar-to-alcohol conversions are proceeding. Each sake will have a target number as the final *nihonshu-do*, but that is really just one facet of a wide range of factors and decisions that go into making a sake what it is.

Somewhere along the line, some brewers began to put this information on labels, and after a while it became laden with undue importance.

Putting the *nihonshu-do* on the label is **neither required nor regulated**. Rarely is it listed on the label for anything but premium sake, and even then it is listed perhaps half the time. No one really hides the number from the public (it is available for almost any sake on the internet, should you want to work that hard), but many do not consider the *nihonshu-do* relevant information for customers.

I myself never actively look for it, yet neither would I shield my eyes should it come into my field of vision when scanning a label. It's just not that

今日の平均的な「日本酒度」は、＋4くらいだ。これは安定した平均値で、とても多くの酒の「日本酒度」が、この数値の前後に集中する。だがこのことが、この数値はどうも頼りにならないと思う、もう一つの理由である。

　甘さと辛さを評価するための、見た目にはもっとましな数値が日本で開発されている。これは「日本酒度」と酸性度の測定値を数学的に組み合わせたものである。この数値のほうが、甘さと辛さを示せる可能性がほんの少し高いが、あまり採用されていない（つまり、だれも使っていない）。

　ここでの要点は、「日本酒度」は興味深く、利用しやすい情報だが、**あまり重要視しないのがベスト**だということだろう。お酒を選ぶ際、考えに入れるほどの価値はない。甘いか辛いかは考えるべきことかもしれない。しかし繰り返していうが、「日本酒度」だけでは、極端な表示でない限り大して参考にならないのだ。

　では、どうしたらわかるのか？　味わってみたらいいのだ！　ほとんどの酒は、甘さでも辛さでも、ほかの特徴でも度を超えることはない。また、甘さや辛さより目立つ重要な特徴が、数えきれないほどあるのだ。

　お酒について説明を聞き、いちかばちか、自分で飲

important, that's all.

The average *nihonshu-do* these days is about +4. This is a solid and strong average because many, many sake's *nihonshu-do* values congregate around that figure. This is yet another reason I find it somewhat undependable.

An ostensibly better measurement for assessing sweet and dry has been developed in Japan using a mathematical combination of the *nihonshu-do* and the measured acidity together. While this holds minimally better potential for indicating sweet or dry, it has not been enthusiastically embraced (read: no one is using it).

Perhaps the main point here is that although the *nihonshu-do* is interesting and readily available information, it is best to **not place too much importance on it**. It is certainly not worth factoring into a decision on which sake to choose. Sweet or dry may be something to consider, but to reiterate, the *nihonshu-do* alone will not tell you much about that except in its extreme manifestations.

So how are we to know, then? Just taste it! Most sake is not extreme in sweetness, dryness, or any other aspect. There are countless aspects of a sake that are more prominent and important than sweetness or a lack thereof.

Ask about a sake, take a chance, taste and smell it

んでみて香りをかぎ、感想をメモしておこう。これが最善の方法であるだけでなく、お酒を評価する上で唯一信頼できる方法である。良かれ悪しかれ、ラベルを見ても、瓶の中で何が待ち受けているのかよくわからないのだから。

for yourself, and note your observations. Not only is this the best way, it is surely the only dependable way to assess a sake. For better or worse, nothing on the label will tell you very much about what awaits you inside.

5. 吟醸

「お酒について一言だけ覚えるなら、『吟醸』にしてください。『吟醸』酒は最高級の酒です。ラベルのどこかに『吟醸』という文字が書かれていたら、**日本酒全体で最高の10％に入る酒を飲んでいることになります**」

わたしはこの言葉を、お酒に興味を持ち、すぐに楽な気持ちで飲んでみたい人たちに向けて、何度唱えてきたかわからない。あまりに単純化しすぎているように見えるかもしれないが、わたしはこの方針を支持している。これには効き目がある。目的は達成できるのだ。セミナーを終えたり記事を読んだりした人たちは、レストランやパブや酒屋に入ると、日本酒通のように思ってもらえる。少なくとも無知だと思われる心配はない。さらに、お酒を注文したり買ったりしても、がっかりすることはほとんどない。この決まり文句は、**お酒を大勢の人にとって近づきやすいものにし、**そうでなければ飲もうとしない人々を、こちらの世界へ招き入れるのだ。

だから、わたしはこの方針を支持する。

しかし、まったく真実というわけではない。それどころか、真実に近くさえないのだ。

5. *Ginjo*

"If you remember one word about sake, let that word be *ginjo*. *Ginjo* sake is super-premium sake; if you drink something with the word *ginjo* written somewhere on the label, you will be drinking **a sake in the top 10 percent of all sake made.**"

I cannot tell you how many times I have intoned those words, directed at people interested in sake who want to start to enjoy it immediately and without undue effort. As overly simplistic as it might seem, I stand by that line. It works; it achieves its purpose. People walk away from a seminar or article and can walk into a restaurant, pub, or retailer and sound like sake cognoscenti, or at least not have to worry about sounding foolish. At the same time they can order or buy sake and know that the chances of being disappointed are slim. The formula makes **sake approachable to the masses** and brings into the fold folks who might otherwise never try sake.

So I stand by that line.

But it ain't the entire truth. In fact, it ain't even close.

ここで、「吟醸」という言葉は、この等級の名称に入る4つの種類すべてを指している。「吟醸」と「純米吟醸」、そしてもっと上の一対である「大吟醸」と「純米大吟醸」だ（「大吟醸」は、「とびきりの吟醸」と覚えておけばいい）。思い出してほしいが、「純米」という言葉がなければ、一定の工程でアルコールが添加されている。（詳細は、p.54「『純米』と『純米』でない酒」の章を参照）。少々まぎらわしい用語かもしれないが、この4つの種類をまとめて、「吟醸」、または「吟醸酒」と呼んでいる。たしかに、「吟醸」酒は今日の市場の約10％を占めている。そしてまさに最高級であり、すばらしい品であり、一般にほかの名称の酒より高価である。しかし、この名称の酒だけが飲むに値するわけではないし、だれもが最初にこれを選ぶとは限らないのだ。

　どういうわけで、技術的に最高のものを、だれもが飲みたがるとは限らないのか？　それは、この格付けは酒の性質を表すものであって、だれの好みにも合うとか、いつも喜ばれるもの、というわけではないからだ。言いかえれば、「吟醸」は軽やかで、**繊細で、香り高く、酸味と土臭さは少ない**。言っておくが、すべての「吟醸」がそうだとは限らない——たっぷりこくがあって、土臭いものもある。だが一般に、「吟醸」は香り高く繊細なのが特徴となっている。そうだ、だから見事な技術と、精米歩合の高い高価な米、多大な製造時間と労力を必要とし、そのため値段も高い。だがそれでも、もっと骨太で、土臭い、香りの少ない酒を好

Here, the word *ginjo* refers to all four subclasses of this grade: *ginjo* and *junmai ginjo*, and the even better duo of *daiginjo* and *junmai daiginjo* (just remember that *daiginjo* is "*ginjo* to die for"). Recall that if the word *junmai* is *not* there, some alcohol has been added as an accepted part of the process. (See the chapter on *junmai* vs. non-*junmai* on page 55, for more.) Mildly confusing nomenclature though it may be, these four types together are collectively called *ginjo* or *ginjo-shu*. Indeed, *ginjo* sake makes up about 10 percent of the market today. And yes, it is super premium, it is great stuff, and it is generally more expensive than other grades of sake. But it is not the only grade of sake worth drinking, and it's not everyone's first choice.

Why in the world would the technically best stuff not be what everyone wants to drink? Because it is a classification that has its own style and nature, and that might not be what appeals to everyone, or what appeals at all times. In other words, *ginjo* can be **light, delicate, and aromatic, low in acidity and earthiness**. Not all *ginjo*, mind you—some are plenty rich and earthy. But in general, as a style, *ginjo* is aromatic and delicate. Yes, it calls for great technical skill, expensive rice that has been highly milled, and more time and effort to produce, hence the higher price tag. Nevertheless, there are those who prefer

む人たちがいるのだ。

「『吟醸』、お呼びでない」と彼らは言う。

この主張は一面では、「吟醸」の性質を表している。多くの人が「吟醸」は「うんざりする」とか、**香りが鼻につく**と言う。純米酒や本醸造酒のような、労働者向きの酒を好む人々もいるのだ。とくにゆっくり座って何杯か飲もうとしているとき、「吟醸」は──「大吟醸」はなおさら──1杯目のあとでは香りがきつすぎるという人がいる。みんなではないが、そういう人もいるのだ。また日本酒愛好家のなかには、**酒盛りには低い等級の酒のほうが向いている**と感じる人がいる。みんなではないが、そういう人もいるのだ。

好みは年齢とともに、また慣れてくるにつれて、変わるのかもしれない。「『吟醸』、お呼びでない」の支持者には、年配の紳士が多いようだ。わたしの好みも、この四半世紀の間に、**地味な酒**に引かれるようになってきた。「『吟醸』、お呼びでない」は、人生における自然な進歩なのかもしれない。

別の見方をすれば、ほかの名称の酒を飲むことが、どんなにおもしろく、値打ちがあり、楽しいかということだ。わたしがはじめに日本酒にのめりこんだとき、「吟醸」に「すごく」のめりこみ、「吟醸」を味わうことしか興味がなかった。実際、酒蔵や企業などを訪れたときも、このことで何度かたしなめられた。「まっすぐ『吟醸』のところに行ってましたね！」と言われ、経験の浅いぼんくらだと、やんわりとほのめかされたものだ。

sake that is more big-boned, earthy, or less aromatic.

"*Ginjo*, schminjo," they say.

One side of this argument is the nature of *ginjo* itself. Many say *ginjo* will "tire you out," or that **the aromatics are cloying**. Some folks prefer more of a workingman's sake, like a *junmai-shu* or even a *honjozo*. Especially when planning to sit down and drink several glasses, some find that *ginjo*—and even more so, *daiginjo*—have aromatics that can be overpowering after the first glass. Not all, but some. Some sake aficionados feel **lower grades tend to make better session sake**. Not all, but some.

It may be too that preferences change with age, as they are wont to do. Many of the "*ginjo*, schminjo" adherents seem to be older gentlemen. My own preferences have gravitated toward **less ostentatious sake** over the last quarter century. *Ginjo*, schminjo may be a natural progression in life.

The other side of the coin is just how interesting, worthwhile, and enjoyable it can be to drink sake of other grades. When I first got into sake, I got *way* into *ginjo*, and it was all I was interested in trying. In fact, as I spent time with brewers and other industry types, I was chided for this more than once. "You just went straight for the *ginjo* there, didn't ya!" I'd be told, lightly implying that I was an inexperienced simpleton.

その優しいジョークは良い効果をもたらし、おかげで自分の酒の世界を広げようと思うようになった。また、酒蔵やその土地について学ぶ最善の方法は、**できるだけいろんな種類のものを飲んでみることだ**と、次第に気づくようになったのだ。「本醸造」酒は驚くほどおいしいことがあるし、「普通酒」はどの名称の酒よりも、その土地の酒について多くのことを教えてくれる。味見する価値は十分にある。「吟醸」しか飲まないと決めていると、お酒の世界のすばらしさの90％を切り捨てることになるのだ。

　「吟醸」嫌いの人も、たしかにいる。「吟醸」の造り方や、定義や、特別な理由をよく知らない偏屈な人たちがいて、さきほど述べた大勢の年配の紳士たちもその中に入ると思う。「吟醸」についてわざわざ学んだり、酒について熟知していないことを匂わせたりするよりも、知っているもの、つまり「本醸造」や、「吟醸」以外のほかの酒にこだわって、「『吟醸』、お呼びでない」を呪文のように繰り返すのだ。

　誤解しないでほしいが、わたしは「吟醸」が大好きである。傑出したものであり、**杜氏たちの技術の極み**だといえる。わたしもとてもよく飲んでいる。ここで言いたいのは、お酒を試すのにすぐ「吟醸」へ向かうのはかまわないが、どうかその名称だけにこだわらないでほしい、ということだ。

　海外であった日本酒奨励のための試飲会のことを思い出す。グラスに酒を注いでいると、ひとりの女性が

That good-natured joking had a positive effect and encouraged me to expand my sake horizons. Also, over time I realized that the best way to learn about any given brewer or region was to **taste as wide a range of types as possible**. *Honjozo* sake can be surprisingly wonderful; *futsu-shu* can teach more about the regional styles of sake than most other grades. It is all worth trying and drinking. Limiting oneself to *ginjo* is cutting off 90 percent of the wonders of the world of sake.

Surely there are those with *ginjo*-phobia. Some codgers don't really know what makes *ginjo* what it is, what defines it, and what makes it special, and I count many an aforementioned older gentleman among that number. Rather than take the time to learn about it, or hint at anything less than a complete understanding of the sake world, they stick with what they know, be it *honjozo* or another non-*ginjo* grade, and recite the mantra "*ginjo*, schminjo."

Don't get me wrong: I love *ginjo*. It can be outstanding and is **the pinnacle of the brewer's craft**. I enjoy plenty of it. All I am saying is while it is okay to immediately gravitate toward *ginjo* to check it out, by all means don't limit yourself to only sake of that grade.

I recall being at one promotional tasting overseas, and up came a woman who asked for the most

やってきて、最も高価な「大吟醸」を飲みたいと言った。それどころか、横に並んだ蔵元にも、同じことを言っているのが聞こえた。「わたしは最高のものしか飲まないの」と、女性は信念を持って語った。「だれの意見で最高なのですか？」とか、「何を基準にしてですか？」とか尋ねる間もなく、彼女は次の「最高」のもの、たぶん次の「大吟醸」を求めてほかの列へ並びに走り去った。

　自分がおいしいと思えば、その酒はおいしいのである。自分にとって最高においしい酒が、最高の酒なのだ。

　「吟醸」、お呼びでない。

expensive *daiginjo* we were pouring. In fact, I had heard her ask the same thing of the brewer next to me. "I only drink the best," she explained with conviction. Before I had a chance to ask "In whose opinion?" or "Based on what criteria?" she had scampered off to the next "best" one down the line, presumably the next *daiginjo*.

If it tastes good to you to you, it is good. The one that tastes the best to you is the best.

Ginjo, schminjo.

6. お酒の純粋さ

お酒はグルテンを含んでいないだろうか？ お酒は純植物性だろうか？

お酒は、その**純粋さ**ゆえに**歓迎される**ことが多い。何と言っても、米と、「麹」菌と、水で造るからだ。ああ、それに、多くの酒は純粋な蒸留エチルアルコールを添加して造られる。だが保存料は使わないので、亜硫酸塩剤は入っていないし、醸造工程を終えたら水と「粕」(p.152参照)以外は加えない。

でも、お酒はグルテンを含んでいないだろうか？ また、純植物性だろうか？ こういう関心は今日ますます大きくなっている。そしてお酒には、その問題について喜ばしい可能性があるのだ。

2つとも簡潔に答えれば、「はい、お酒はグルテンを含まないし、純植物性です」となる。だが実際は、すべての酒がどこでもいつでもその制約に従って造られていると、100％保証することは不可能だ。ただ、ほとんどの人や状況に対しては、2つとも満たしていると答えられる。

まず、グルテンの問題から始めよう。日本酒は米を

6. Sake Purity

Is it gluten free? Is it vegan?

Sake is often **hailed for its purity**. After all, it is made from rice, *koji* mold, and water. Oh, and much of it is made with the addition of some pure, distilled ethyl alcohol. However, no preservatives are used, sake is sulfite free, and once the brewing process is completed nothing can be added but water and *kasu* (see page 153).

But is sake gluten free? And is it vegan? These are growing concerns these days, and sake holds great potential as something that people with these concerns can enjoy.

The short answer to both is "Yes, sake is both gluten free and vegan." However, the truth is that it is not feasible to absolutely, 100 hundred percent guarantee that all sake made everywhere at any time conforms to these restrictions. But for almost all people and situations, we can say yes, it conforms to both.

Let's start with the question of gluten. Sake is

醸造したものだ。米だけが使用される穀物であり、唯一の発酵原料である。米はグルテンを含まない。ここまでは大丈夫だ。ほかの原料は水、「麹」菌（「アスペルギルス・オリーゼ」）、酵母だけである。もしこの材料しか使わないなら——すべての純米酒のように——、そう、グルテンはまったく含んでいないと言うことができる。よし決まった。**以上証明終わりだ**。

グルテンが気になるなら、ラベルに「純米」の文字があるものを飲もう。その酒はグルテンを含んでいないからだ。

しかし、「純米」でない酒はどうだろう？「普通酒」や「本醸造」、「純米」でない「吟醸」や「大吟醸」は？ これらには、少量の純粋な蒸留アルコールが添加されている。このアルコールは何からできているのだろうか？ それでもグルテンを含まないと言えるだろうか？

結論から先に言おう。ちょっと、ちょっと！ エチルアルコールだよ！ 化学式は C_2H_6O だ。原料に関係なく、**お酒に添加されるアルコールは何度も蒸留されているから、エチルアルコール以外の何物でもない**。少なくともわたしはそう思う。だが、これで満足しない人もいるかもしれない。

では、その原料について見てみよう。ほとんど例外なく、「純米」でない酒に添加するアルコールは安価な輸入物で、サトウキビを蒸留したものである。そしてサトウキビはグルテンを含んでいない。ただし、自前の純米酒（グルテンなし）からアルコールを蒸留し、

brewed rice; rice is the only grain used and the only fermentable material. Rice does not contain any gluten. So far, so good. The only other ingredients are water, *koji* mold (*Aspergillus oryzae*), and yeast. If a sake uses only these ingredients—as all *junmai* sake types do—then yes, we can say that it is absolutely gluten free. Done. **Quod erat demonstrandum**.

If glutens are a concern, drink something with the word *junmai* on the label, because that is a gluten-free sake.

But what about the non-*junmai* types? What of *futsu-shu*, *honjozo*, and the non-*junmai ginjo* and *daiginjo* grades? These have had a bit of pure distilled alcohol added. From where does this alcohol come? Can this be said to be gluten-free too?

First things first: Psst! It's ethyl alcohol! The chemical formula is C_2H_6O. Regardless of its source, the **alcohol added to sake has been distilled over and over** so that it is nothing more than ethyl alcohol, at least in my thinking. However, this might not satisfy some people.

Next, let's look at the source. Almost without exception, the alcohol added to non-*junmai* sake is cheap and imported, having been distilled from sugar cane, which contains no gluten. I'm aware of a couple whacked-out (in a good way) brewers who

それを加えて酒造りをしている、もう正気とは思えない（いい意味でだが）酒蔵がいくつかあることも知っている。

　大麦や、グルテンを含むほかの穀物から蒸留したアルコールを使う酒蔵が、絶対どこにもないと断言することはできない。だがそのアルコールは──ウィスキーと違って──、エチルアルコールだけになるまで蒸留されるので問題はないだろう。ただ、過去に大麦ではなかったという保証はないのだ。

　とはいえ、はっきりした理由で、ほぼ間違いなく保証することができる。

　サトウキビ由来のアルコールはきわめて安く、それに対して大麦由来のアルコールは高価なのだ。そんなアルコールに高い金を払うまともな酒蔵はないだろう。化学的にまったく同じなのに、いちばん安いものを使わないというのは経済的に意味がない。だから、「純米」でない酒がグルテンを含んでいないという完璧な保証はないが、実際にはあると言ってもいい。もっとも安価なアルコールは、大麦ではなくサトウキビからできるからだ。

　最後に、「普通酒」について考えよう。もっとも安い酒で、アルコールと、ときには糖分を加えて造られる。ここには問題があるかもしれない！　甘味をもたらしているものが、米由来の「麹」だったら大丈夫だ。しかし、甘味をもたらすものが「水あめ」のときがあり、こ

actually distill alcohol from their own (gluten-free) *junmai-shu* and add that to their products.

I cannot say with airtight certainty that no brewer anywhere ever uses alcohol distilled from barley or another gluten-containing grain. This should not matter as—unlike whiskey—the alcohol has been distilled to the point that only ethyl alcohol remains. But there is no guarantee that it was not barley once upon a time.

However, I can *almost* guarantee it, for a very clear reason.

Sugar cane-based ethyl alcohol is extremely cheap, whereas barley-based ethyl alcohol is expensive. No brewer in his or her right mind is going to pay any more than he or she has to for this stuff. Economically it would make no sense for a brewer to use anything but the cheapest variety, since it is chemically identical. So, although there is no absolute guarantee that non-*junmai* sake is gluten-free, there practically is, because the cheapest alcohol comes from sugar cane, not barley.

Finally, consider *futsu-shu*, the cheapest sake, made with both added alcohol and sometimes sugars. Here we might have a problem! That sweetening agent may have been from rice-based *koji*, in which case we are fine. But there is a chance that the sweetening agent

れは「もち米」という、とくにデンプンの多い米から造られるのだ。また、デンプンから糖への糖化を促進するために、大麦の麦芽を加えられているかもしれないのだ。言っておくが、ほんの少しである。しかし、ゼロではない。

つまり、「普通酒」には甘味を加えたものがあるということだ。甘味には米由来の「麹」もある。しかし、ラベルを見ても糖分の原料はわからない。だから、「普通酒」には非常に少量の大麦が入っているかもしれないのだ。

もうひとつ、注意が必要なことがある。果物の香りや、ほかの風味をつけた酒はどうなのだろう？ 添加する香料については？ そういう酒もグルテンを含まないと言えるだろうか？

日本では、お酒に果物の香りを加えることはできない。もし加えたら、その製品は法的に日本酒ではなくなる。税法上、本物の酒ではない。だから、果物風味の日本酒は日本には存在しない（人気のある「梅酒」もそうだ。日本酒だと思っている人が多いが、法的にはそうではない）。だが、この法律は海外で造られた果物風味の酒には適用されない。もちろん、グルテンを含まないかどうか知りたい人のために、製造者は必要な情報を持っていることだろう。

さて、日本酒は純植物性ということについてはどうだろう？ これは少し厄介かもしれない。いわゆる「込み入った問題」だ。

was *mizu-ame*, which is mostly made from an extra-starchy rice called *mochigome*. Some barley-based malt *may* have also been added to get the starch-to-sugar conversion going. Just a bit, mind you, but not zero.

The point here is that **some *futsu-shu* has sweeteners added to it**. Some of that is from rice-based *koji*. But we cannot tell from the label the source of these sugars, so it is possible that the *futsu-shu* was made with a *minuscule* amount of barley.

One more caution: What of fruit-flavored or other flavored sake? What about the added flavorings? Can we say that those are gluten free?

In Japan, **fruit flavors cannot be added to sake**. Once you do, the product is no longer legally sake. It is not a purist thing, it is a legal and tax thing. So no fruit-flavored sake exists in Japan (this includes popular sake-based *ume-shu*, or plum "sake," which many think is sake but legally is not). However, these laws do not apply to fruit-flavored sake made in other countries. Certainly, the producers would have the necessary information for those who need to confirm whether these sakes are indeed gluten free.

What about sake being vegan? This one may prove a bit trickier, or, as they say, "It's complicated."

動物性の製品はどんな形でも、日本酒の製造で使用されることはない。だが酒を醸造した後、**たいてい木炭を使って濾過する**のだが、その木炭を除くのに動物性のゼラチンを使用する酒蔵がある。完成品の酒に残ることはないが、一工程で使用されるのだ。

　ほとんどの酒蔵では使用しないが、ラベルからは容易に判断できない。また、すべての酒が木炭による濾過を行っているわけではない。木炭による濾過をしないなら、グルテンも使用されない。木炭での濾過をしない酒は、「無濾過」という名で知られている。

　もしその酒が「純米」の種類なら、使用されているのは米、水、「麹」菌だけなので、純植物性の基準に適合すると言える。

　これでひとつの結論が出た。「純米」、「純米吟醸」、「純米大吟醸」か、「無濾過」であれば、その酒は純植物性なのである。

　もし「純米」タイプでなくても、つまり、製造工程で少量のアルコールが加えられていても、そのアルコールを蒸留するときに、植物性でないものは加えない。しかし結局、問題は動物性のゼラチンも使用されるかどうかにかかってくる。

　もうひとつ注意すべきことがある。ほとんどの酒の製造に、乳酸が使用される。だが、そのような乳酸は動物性の原料からでなく、乳酸菌から工業的に造られている。これは同じように使用される乳糖にも当ては

No animal products of any type are used in the production of sake. However, after sake has been brewed, **it is usually filtered with charcoal**, and some breweries then use an animal-based gelatin to help remove the charcoal. This does not end up in the final sake, but it is used at some stage of the process.

Most brewers do *not* do this, but one cannot easily tell from the label. Also, not all sake is charcoal filtered. If a sake has not been charcoal filtered, then the gelatin would not have been used. Sake that has not been charcoal filtered is known as *muroka*.

If a sake is of the *junmai* variety, we can say that it conforms to vegan standards because only rice, water, and *koji* mold were used.

This leads us to one safe haven: if a sake is a *junmai*, *junmai ginjo*, or *junmai daiginjo*, and if it is *muroka*, then yes, that sake is vegan.

If a sake is not a *junmai* type, in other words, if a bit of alcohol was added during the process, it would still be vegan since nothing involved in distilling the added alcohol would disqualify it. But in the end it would still depend on whether or not animal-based gelatin was also used.

There is one more caveat: lactic acid is used in the production of most sake. But such lactic acid is industrially produced from lactic bacteria, not from animal sources. This also applies to any lacto-sugars

まることで、やはり動物由来ではない。

　要するに、ラベルに「純米」という文字があるものはどれでも、たしかにグルテンは含まれていないのだ。高級酒はほとんどそうである。「普通酒」は信用できないかもしれないが、いずれにせよ、「普通酒」をたくさん飲みたいとは思わないだろう。

　また、木炭による濾過をしていない酒（「無濾過」だが、ラベルに表示されているとは限らない）は、間違いなく純植物性である。動物由来のゼラチンを使用している少数の酒だけは、純植物性とは言えないだろう。だから、「純米」でない酒でも、純植物性でありうる。とはいえ、ゼラチンが使われているかどうかは、ラベルを見てもわからない。

　上述したことは、期待するほど単純明快ではないかもしれないが、ほとんどの酒は十中八九グルテンを含まず、純植物性である。ただし、絶対に保証できるというわけではない。

that might be used as well; they are not animal based.

In summary: anything with the word *junmai* on the label is sure to be gluten free. Any premium sake is almost certain to be. *Futsu-shu* may be dodgy, but you don't likely want to drink much *futsu-shu* anyway.

Any sake that is not charcoal filtered (*muroka*, but this is not always indicated on the label) is sure to be vegan. Only the very few that use animal-based gelatin would not be vegan, so even non-*junmai* sake could be vegan too. However, we cannot know from the label if such gelatins were used.

While the above may not be as clear-cut or as simple as we would like it to be, most sake is *highly likely* to be both gluten free and vegan, although this cannot be absolutely guaranteed.

7. 酒瓶の日付と、「どのくらいで古いのか?」

　新鮮さが大切だ！ お酒に関して、「新鮮なほどいい」といえば少し誇張に聞こえるかもしれないが、それでもやはり、その酒瓶がどのくらい経っているのか知る必要がある。**ラベルから得られる情報は、すべてのことを教えてはくれない**──すべてには程遠いのだ！ しかし、たいていは事足りるし、いずれにしても理解しておく価値はある。

　お酒の瓶には、たいていラベルの下の隅に日付がついている。だが、これは何の日付だろう？ お酒が生まれた日だろうか、または、醸造が終わった日だろうか？ もしかしたら、いちばん飲みごろの日？ じつはまったく別のものだ。そして予想通り、あいまいにぼかされているのだ。

　どう見ても、瓶の日付は「蔵」から出荷された日である。ここで大事なのは、「どう見ても」という言葉だ。

　実際には、酒蔵は法律上、**お酒を瓶詰めしたときに日付をつけなければならない**。瓶詰めしたらすぐに出荷するだろうと考えてのことだ。これは長い間行われてきたやり方である。タンクに貯蔵し、出荷の直前に瓶詰めし、税金を支払う。間違いない、税金に関する

7. The Date on the Bottle and "How Long Is Too Long?"

Freshness is important! When it comes to sake, while "the fresher the better" might be a little bit of an exaggeration, we still need to know how old a given bottle might be. **The information we can garner from the label will not tell us everything**—far from it! But usually it is enough, and in any event is very worth understanding.

Sake bottles do have a date on them, usually in the lower corner of the label. But what is this date? The day on which the sake was born, or on which brewing was completed? Is it the best-enjoyed-by date, perhaps? It is actually something else altogether. And not surprisingly, it is shrouded in vagueness.

For all intents and purposes, the date on the bottle is the date that the sake was shipped from the *kura*. The key phrase here is *for all intents and purposes*.

In actuality, brewers legally **must affix the date when the sake is bottled**, with the thinking being that they will ship it soon after bottling it. This is the way things had long been done: store it in a tank, bottle it just before shipping, and pay taxes on it. And make

ことなのだ。だが、ちょっと脱線してみよう。

さて、お酒は瓶詰めしたときに日付をつけるのだが、出荷する直前に瓶詰めするのなら、どう見ても、その日付は出荷の日だと考えられる。だが瓶詰めしてもすぐ出荷されないお酒もある。たとえば酒蔵が一度に大量に瓶詰めしたら、その日に出ていく瓶もあるし、何ヵ月も残る瓶もあるかもしれない。わざと見逃されたというお酒もあるだろう。

しかし、タンクより瓶で貯蔵するほうが、ますます一般的になってきている。とくに高級酒ではそうである。これによってお酒は**きめ細かく繊細な舌触り**になると、多くの杜氏たちは感じている。そこで規則は曲げられて、日付は瓶詰めしたときにつけなければならないが、瓶で熟成させる場合は別ということになっているのだ。その場合、瓶にラベルを貼ることは許可されていない。**熟成の工程から出てきてラベルを貼るときに、日付がつけられる。**

つまり、瓶で熟成して貯蔵庫から出したときに、ラベルを貼って、日付をつけ、ようやく出荷するということだ。それならどう見ても、日付は出荷する日だと考えられる。少なくとも、わたしはそう思う。

だから、瓶の日付は瓶詰めした日だ。そうでないとき以外は。

こういうわけで、「どう見ても」をつけておきたい。そして、瓶の日付は、その酒が「蔵」から出荷されたと

no mistake, it is really all about taxes. But I digress.

So, if a sake is dated when bottled, but bottled just before it is shipped, then for all intents and purposes the date can be considered to be the shipping date. However, some sake are not shipped just after bottling. If a brewer bottles in huge lots, for example, some might go out that day but the rest might not go out for months. Some sake will fall through the cracks of those intents and purposes.

However, more and more commonly, sake is stored in bottles rather than tanks; this is especially true for premium sake. Many brewers feel this **gives sake a more fine-grained and delicate texture**. So the rules have been bent to read that the date must be applied when you bottle the sake, unless you plan to age it in that bottle. In that case, the brewer is not permitted to label the bottle. The date is applied **when the sake comes out of maturation and is labeled**.

This means that when a sake is aged in a bottle and is taken out of storage, labeled, dated, and finally shipped, then for all intents and purposes the date can be considered to be the shipping date. Or at least, that's how I see it.

So, the date on the bottle is the bottling date. Unless it isn't.

This is why I prefer the *for all intents and purposes* addendum, and hold that the date on a bottle of sake

き（何年何月）を示しているのだと確信している。

　この日付ではわからないことは何なのかも、知っておこう。これを見ても、その酒が出来てどのくらい経つかわからない。酒蔵は望んでいる味にするために、それぞれ違う期間で熟成させる。軽やかな酒を造る酒蔵は約４ヵ月しか熟成させず、土臭い酒を造る酒蔵は出荷前に１年半寝かせるかもしれない。どちらにしても、求めていた味になるまで熟成させたら、**すぐに飲んでほしい**と思っている。しかし、どちらも瓶には同じ日付がついていて、醸造されてから１年以上の差があるかもしれないのだ。

　日付を見ても瓶で熟成したのか、タンクで熟成したのかわからないし、どのくらい熟成させたのかも全然わからない。いつまで味が著しく変わらずにもつのかわからないし、いつまでに飲めばいいのかもわからない。日付は瓶詰めされた日にすぎないのだ。そうでないとき以外は。

　日付が大して当てにならないことがわかったところで、では結局、お酒はどのくらいで、もう古いといえばいいのだろう？　新鮮で最高の状態のときに飲むには、日付からどのくらい後に飲めばいいのだろう？　だれもが単純明快な答えを求めているのはわかっているが、じつはそういうものはない。

　どのくらいで古いかは、多くの要因によって決まるのだ。どのように出荷されたか？　冷蔵コンテナに入

indicates about when (month and year) the sake was shipped from the *kura*.

Note, too, **what this date does *not* tell you**. It does not tell you how old the sake is. Different brewers mature sake for different periods of time to achieve the desired flavor profile. A brewer of a lighter sake might mature it for only four months or so, but a brewer of a more earthy style might have the sake sit for a year and a half before shipping. Either way, **they want you to enjoy it immediately** since they matured it to just where they want it. But both might have the same date on the bottle and be over a year apart since being brewed.

The date also does not tell you if the sake was aged in a bottle or a tank, or how long it was aged at all. Nor does it tell you how much time you have before you can expect noticeable changes to the flavor, or by when you should drink it. That date is nothing but the bottling date. Unless it isn't.

Since we know that we cannot trust that date to tell us much, how old is too old? How soon after the printed date should we consume a sake to be assured it is fresh and in prime drinking condition? As much as I know that everyone wants a straight, short, and clear answer, **there isn't one**.

Just how long is too long depends on a whole host of things. How was the sake shipped? In a refrigerated

れてか？（今日ではほとんどそうである）。出荷先でそのように保管されたか？　なま温かい倉庫か、または冷蔵庫か？「蔵」を出てから、小売店の明るい光の下にどのくらい置かれているか？

　さらにまた、お酒自体のことも考えなければならない。熟成しても大丈夫な種類だろうか？　同じ期間同じ場所に保管されていても、ほかと比べてさほど変化しないものもある。アルコール分、酸味、「純米」か「純米」でないか、また精米歩合も影響する。たとえば、こくがあって少し酸味が強く、アルコール分が高い酒は、軽やかで繊細で香り高い「大吟醸」よりも長くもつ。また辛口の酒は、ブドウ糖やアミノ酸の多い酒に比べて変化が少ない。

　一般的に、いや、どのお酒でも、何日、何週間、何ヵ月で、自動的に絶対「古くなる」という決まった期限はないのだ。だが、どうしても簡単な答えが必要なら、**経験からいって18ヵ月程度は大丈夫**だろう。ただし、これは割り引いて考え、絶対の数字だと思わないでほしい。製造者が良心的で、輸入者も誠実で正しく保管してくれたと想定しての数字である。

container? (Almost all sake is these days.) How was it stored when it got to its destination? In a warmish warehouse or a refrigerated one? How much time since it left the *kura* has been spent under the bright lights of the retailer?

Then there is the sake itself to consider. Is it a style that will stand up to maturation or not? Some sake will change much less than other sake over the same time period and under the same storage conditions. Alcohol content, acidity, whether it is *junmai* or non-*junmai*, and the milling rate all affect this. As an example, a robust sake with a slightly higher-than-normal acidity and even a slightly higher-than-usual alcohol will last much longer than a light, delicate, aromatic *daiginjo*. A dry sake will exhibit much less change than a sake with more glucose and amino acid content.

What cannot be said about sake in general, or even any one sake, is that after a certain number of days, weeks, or months, a sake is automatically and definitely "too old." If I had to give a short answer, a **rule of thumb**, I would say **sake is good for no more than eighteen months**. Still, take this with a grain of salt, and don't consider it a hard-and-fast number. This rule assumes the producer is good and the importer is conscientious enough to have stored it properly.

では、わからないときはどうすればいいのか？　味見してみよう。味見の経験を重ねれば、古くなったらどんな味がするかわかるようになる。わざと熟成させたお酒を味見しても、その変化がわかる。だが、古くなってしまった酒を味見するほうがいいだろう。瓶の中での長い時間が、お酒にどのように表れるかを学び、その知識を応用しよう。これが、「どのくらいで古いのか？」を知るためのもっとも確実で——そしてもっとも楽しい——方法なのだ。

　だれもが単純明快な答えを求める。でも、そんなものはない。これが真実なのだ。

So what should you do if you are not sure? Taste it. With enough tasting experience, you can learn to taste when sake is too old. You can do this by deliberately aging sake and seeing what happens to it, but perhaps it is better to taste sake that you know has gotten old. Learn how too much time in a bottle manifests itself in sake and apply that knowledge. That is the surest—and most enjoyable—way to know "How old is too old?"

Everyone wants one straight, short answer. But it doesn't exist. That is the truth.

8. 温めたお酒

お酒を温めるか、冷やすか、この二択は最大の問題だろう。どのお酒をどちらにしたらいいか、またその理由について確信の持てない人が多い。それに加えて、人が何というか、どのように温めるか、さらには個人的好みという避けられない複雑な問題もある。これでは気が遠くなりそうだ。

そのため、お酒をすすめる人たちのなかには、「おいしい酒は冷やしたほうがいい、まずい酒は温めたらいい」と、**両極端に分けて簡略化してしまう人が多い**。でも、それほど単純なものではないし、この意見は少しも正しくない。

じつは伝統的にではないにしても、歴史的には、**お酒は冷やすより温めて出されることが多かった**。歴史的記録や酒器を見ると、10世紀までさかのぼっても、お酒は温めて飲まれていたようだ。おそらく、その習慣は隣国の中国からやってきたのだろう。中国では、冷たいものより、温かいものを食べたり飲んだりするほうが健康的だと考えられていた。冷たいものは体の芯を冷やすと思われていたのだ。

ところが、「吟醸」のように香り高く繊細な高級酒が

8. Warm Sake

The "hot versus cold" dichotomy may be one of sake's biggest distractions. Many people are unsure **which is the right choice for which sake, and why that is**. Add to that the questions of how one can tell, how to warm the sake, and the inevitable complexities that come along with personal preferences, and it can all be daunting.

This is why many sake promoters **have oversimplified things by polarizing the answer** into "good sake should be chilled, bad sake can be heated." Not only is it not that simple, but that statement is not even close to being correct.

It is true that historically, if not traditionally, **more sake was served warm than cold**. Historical records and vessels show that sake was enjoyed warm as far back as the 10th century. It is very likely that the practice made it to Japan via neighboring China, where eating and drinking warmed things has always been considered healthier than eating cold things, which were thought to chill the center of the body.

However, as premium sake like *ginjo* developed

開発されるようになると(1980年代の後半ごろ)、**高級酒は少し冷やして飲む**という考え方に勢いがついてきた。なぜだろう？ それは、お酒を温めることで、杜氏(とうじ)たちが苦労して引き出した特色が失われてしまうかもしれないからだ。高級酒を冷やす習慣は日本で流行し、90年代までには、温めた高級酒は忘れ去られるようになった。少なくとも、再発見してもらえるのを待つようになったのだ。

　この風潮は海外での事情にも影響を与えた。お酒の輸入業者は、ワイン愛好家たちの**心と味覚をつかもうと努力**していたが、壁にぶつかることが多かったのだ。
　「お酒なら飲んだことがあるわ。結構よ。興味ないから」
　「そうですか」と答える。「でも、『吟醸』のような高級酒をお飲みになったことがありますか？ これは温めずに、冷やして飲むんです。まえにお飲みになったのとは、まるで違うと保証しますよ！」この作戦のおかげで人々はお酒を味見するようになり、しかもおいしいと言う人が多かったので、目的にかなったわけである。
　しかしそのために、おいしい酒は冷やして飲み、まずい酒は温めて飲むべきだという、簡単すぎてありふれた考え方が広まったのだ。高級酒を少し冷やして飲むのは、お酒を飲みはじめたばかりの人にとっては、目安となるいい方法だ。でも、もうまずい酒など存在

into more aromatic, delicate stuff (in perhaps the late 1980s), the concept of **enjoying premium sake slightly chilled** gained momentum. Why? Because heating sake like that would bludgeon out of existence the traits that the brewers worked so hard to draw out. The practice of chilling premium sake caught on in Japan, and by the '90s, it seemed that premium warm sake was beginning to be forgotten. Or at least it was awaiting rediscovery.

This trend played into what was happening overseas as well. While sake importers **strove to capture the hearts and palates** of the wine-loving world, they often met a brick wall.

"I've had sake. No thanks. Not interested."

"Ah," would come the reply. "But have you had premium sake, like *ginjo*? It is served cold, not hot, and I guarantee you it is different from what you have had before!" This ploy would get folks to taste sake, and often, to appreciate it, so it has served a purpose.

But this led to an all-too-familiar and oversimplified perception that good sake should be enjoyed cold, and less-good sake should be drunk hot. While enjoying premium sake slightly chilled can still be a useful rule of thumb for those just

しないという事実を考えると、この意見の後半部分は疑わしいと言えるだろう。

一番ひどい嘘（誤解？）は、まずい酒は欠点を隠すために温める、ということだろう。自分が造った酒を味見して、あたりを見まわし、「いやあ、こいつはひどい味だな。温めて誤魔化すか」などと言う杜氏（とうじ）は、どこにもいたためしがない。そうとも、わたしはそう思う。お酒は今や、そしてこれまでもずっと、欠点を隠すために温めることなどない。たしかに温めるとある程度効果があるが、それは温める目的ではないのだ。

では、なぜ温めた酒がいたるところに、そして日本中の料理店にあるのだろう？　**お酒の代表のように見えるのはどうしてだろう？**　ひとつには、温めることで味が損なわれるような種類の酒は、市場で占める割合がとても小さいからだ。製造される酒の大部分は、質素で素朴な「食中酒」である。思い出してほしい。フルーティーでないからといって、おいしくないわけではないことを。「『吟醸』、お呼びでない」と言う人もいるのだ。

だからある意味、**温めるほうが伝統的な飲み方であり、伝統はなかなか消えないものだ。**また、ほかの業界と同じように、企業は安い酒をたくさん売ることで利益を得ており、その酒の大部分は、ずっとそうだったというだけの理由で温めて飲まれている。しかも「吟醸」が市場で目立ちだしたのは、80年代前半になっ

getting into sake, the fact that there is almost no bad sake in existence anymore renders the second half of the statement moot.

Perhaps the most egregious of untruths (misconceptions?) out there is that bad sake is heated to cover the flaws. There has never been a brewer that tasted his product, looked around, and said, "Woah, this stuff is *bad*. Let's heat it and fool everyone." Nah, I don't think so. Sake is not now—nor has it ever been—heated to deliberately cover the flaws. Surely heating will accomplish that to some degree, but it was never the objective of warming.

Why then is hot sake everywhere, at every Japanese restaurant around? Why does it **seem to be the go-to sake**? Part of the reason is that only a very small share of the market is the kind of sake that would suffer from warming. The majority of all sake made is still simple, straightforward "table sake." Remember, just because something isn't fruity doesn't mean it isn't good. *Ginjo*, schminjo, say some.

So, in one sense, **warming is more of a traditional way to enjoy sake**, and **tradition dies hard**. And, like any industry, the large players benefit from selling lots of inexpensive product, and much of that is enjoyed hot simply because it always has been. Also, *ginjo* has only been around as a significant presence

てからだ。それ以前の多くの酒は、たしかに温めるのに適している。これらの要因が相まって、温めた酒はなくならないのである。

さて、「吟醸」は少し冷やして飲むのがベストだという一般論は、目的にはかなっているが、真実は愉快なほど複雑で、興味深く、魅力的だ。

温めるのに適した味の酒を温めて飲むと、**人生が変わるような経験をすることがある**。こういう神の顕現を誘うような酒の多くは、高級な「吟醸」である。そう、つまり、温めるとおいしくなる「吟醸」があるのだ。

「吟醸」やほかの酒が温めるに適しているかどうかは、その味わいの特徴でみるしかない。とてもよくあるのが、土臭さ——かなりの苦み、酸味、または甘味とみなされるだろうが、大事なのはこれらが混じり合った風味であること——が、**温めた時に酒を驚くべきものに変えることだ**。だが難しく考える必要はない。辛口で、こくがあり、旨味の多い酒は、温めるとすばらしい別物に変身することもあるのだ。

では、どうやって見分けるのか？ 日本ではよく、製造者がおすすめの温度をラベルに記している。だがこの情報は輸入物にはほとんどない。おそらく製造者ではなく輸入業者が、消費者を悩ませたくないと考えるからだろう。種類では、「山廃（やまはい）」と「生酛（きもと）」（p.172 参照）や熟成酒が温めるのにうってつけだ。

in the market since the early '80s. Much more sake before that period was indeed suited to warming. All of these factors combined have helped hot sake to maintain its presence.

While the generalization that most *ginjo* is best enjoyed slightly chilled serves a purpose, the truth is deliciously more complex, interesting, and appealing.

Warming a sake that has a flavor profile suited to it **can lead to a life-altering experience**. Much of this epiphany-inducing sake is premium *ginjo*. So, yes, there are *ginjo* that can be warmed with delicious results.

What makes a *ginjo*—or any other sake—suited to warming is nothing more than the flavor profile. Very often an earthiness—perhaps characterized by higher bitterness, acidity, or even sweetness, but more importantly the combination of these—**lets a sake meld into something extraordinary when warmed**. But it need not be complex: dry, thick, and/or umami-laden sake can morph into something wonderfully different at warm temperatures too.

How can one tell? Often in Japan the producer will indicate recommended serving temperatures on the label, but this information rarely appears on exported product, probably because the importer—rather than the producer—wants to keep things simple for the customer. In terms of styles, *yamahai* and

じつのところ、一番いいのは試行錯誤することだ。いま飲んでいる酒を何でもいいから、冷やさずに室温で飲んでみよう。それから、室温でおいしかったものを少し温めて飲んでみてほしい。とにかく、破られない規則はないのだから。

この方法のいいところは、とっておきの秘密が見つかるということだ。つまり、**どの酒も、温度が違うとまったく別物のような味がする**ということだ。きっと、どれもがその日その状況で、一番おいしく感じる温度があるだろう。しかも温度による幅広さの魅力に、すっかり魅了されることだろう。「温かい」と「冷たい」だけでは、あまりに選択肢が少なすぎる。昔は、お酒を出すときのさまざまな温度を表す言葉が、日本語にはたくさんあったのだ。しかし今日では、普段使われるのはほんの少しになってしまった。

温かい酒や熱い酒は、一般に「燗酒」、または「お燗」と呼ばれる。「熱燗」は湯気が出るほど熱い酒のことである。一方「ぬる燗」はなまぬるい酒で、高級酒を飲むには、あいまいだが最高にすばらしい温度だ。

さて次に大事なのは、お酒の温め方である。ベストな方法があるだろうか？ もちろん、そんなものはな

kimoto types (see page 173) as well as sake with some maturity are naturals as candidates for warming.

In truth, **the best way to know is trial and error**. Try a sake—any sake that you enjoy—at room temperature rather than chilled. Then take the ones that appealed to you at room temperature and try them a bit warmer. There are no rules except the ones that are constantly being broken anyway.

The advantage to doing things this way is that you will also discover one of the best secrets: **any one given sake will be enjoyable as a different animal at each temperature range**. Sure, each one will have a temperature at which it tastes best to you on that day and in that situation. But its appeal across a range of temperatures will fascinate you. Even just "hot" and "cold" are tremendously limiting. Long ago, there were a dozen words in Japanese used to refer to the wide range of temperatures at which sake might be served. These days, though, very few are used with any regularity.

Warm or hot sake is known generically as *kanzake* or *o-kan*. *Atsukan* means piping-hot sake, whereas *nurukan* refers to more tepid sake, an absolutely wonderful if vague temperature range for enjoying premium sake.

Then there is the *how* of warming sake. Is there one best way? Of course not! But one principle

い！　だが、原則は覚えておくといいだろう。お酒は好みの器に入れて、静かに沸いている湯につけ、時々揺り動かしながら数分間、お好みの温度になるまで温める。その**温度は経験で確かめよう**（つまり、温めて飲んでみよう）。ぐつぐつ沸騰している湯につけるのはよくない。アルコール分が蒸発して、お酒の本来の構造がゆがめられてしまうかもしれない。せっぱ詰まった時は電子レンジでもいいが、適温にするのが難しいし、この方法でもお酒の特徴がいくらか失われそうである（科学的な根拠はないが）。

日本では最近、燗酒が復活してきているようで、**楽しくて実用的な道具・小物・装具が入手できる**。お酒を入れた器を湯の入った容器につける、小型の二重鍋のような安くて簡単な装置もたくさんある。これを使えば、お酒を思いどおりの温度に温めて、保温することもできる。探してみる価値は十分にある！

わたしもかつては、冷やした「吟醸」を崇拝する俗物だった。はじめに高級酒にのめりこんだ頃は、数年間というもの、「吟醸」以外飲まなかったし、冷やしてしか飲まなかった。だが何年も杜氏たちと付き合うう

worth remembering is that sake should be heated by immersing a vessel of choice into just-boiled or simmering water and stirring occasionally for a few minutes until it reaches the desired temperature, **which is verified empirically** (read: taste the stuff as you warm it). It is best not to do it in water that is actively boiling as that can cause some of the alcohol to evaporate, skewing the original make-up of the sake. A microwave oven will work in a pinch, but it is hard to be accurate, and this method also seems to rob the sake of some character (although there are no scientific grounds for this).

There seems to be a modern renaissance in Japan over warmed sake, and **the tools, toys, and accoutrements available these days are both fun and practical**. Many are cheap, simple devices that fit a sake-containing vessel into another that holds hot water, like a miniature double boiler, which warms sake predictably and consistently. These are well worth the search!

I, too, was once a chilled *ginjo* snob. When I first got into premium sake, for several years I drank nothing but *ginjo*, and never any way but chilled. As I spent more time with brewers, though, I was often chided

ちに、想像力のなさを何度もたしなめられたのだ。
　「いいかい、若いの」と言われたのを思い出す。「いい酒とは何か知りたいんだろ？　いい酒はな、冷やしても温めてもどっちでもうまいんだ。そうさ、それがいい酒なんだよ！」自分より数世代も長くこの業界にいる人と、議論する資格はないと思ったわたしは、その言葉を深く胸に刻み込んだ。いやあ、そうして良かったと、心から思っている。

for my lack of imagination.

"Listen, kid," I recall being told. "You wanna know what a good sake is? A good sake is one that can be enjoyed *both* chilled *and* warm. Now *that's* a good sake!" I figured I was not one to argue with someone who had been in this industry several generations longer than me, so I took the words to heart. Man, am I glad I did.

9. にごり酒

　お酒を出している料理店ならどこへ行っても（ともかく日本以外では）、「にごり酒」が、少なくとも1つはメニューに載っているようだ。「にごり酒」はどうやって造るのか？　また、これほど人気があるのはなぜだろう？

　「にごり酒」は、白く濁ったお酒である。じつは、それが「にごり」という言葉の意味だ。(「生酒」のように、「酒」の「さ」は「ざ」になる。会話では、接尾辞の「──ざけ」は省略することが多い)。**中にある濁りは発酵できなかった米のかすであり、完成した酒にわざと残してある。**

　昔、お酒はすべて「にごり」だった。おそらく1000年くらい前まで、発酵後に**酒と米のかすをわざわざ分けようとする者はいなかった**。これがどうして変わったかについて、2、3の話が記録に残っている。

　1つの話はこうだ。現在の兵庫県、かつて酒造りの中心地だった伊丹の酒蔵で、ひとりの蔵人が首になった。失業して不満を抱いた蔵人は、「蔵」へこっそり戻って忍び込むと、仕返しのために、できたての白い酒の酒樽へ大量の木炭の粉を放り込んだ。「これで奴

9. *Nigori*

It seems that everywhere you go, any restaurant (outside of Japan, anyway) that carries sake has at least one *nigorizake* selection. How do they make it and to what does it owe its apparent popularity?

Nigorizake is cloudy sake; in fact, that is what the word *nigori* means. (As with *namazake*, the *s* of "sake" becomes a *z*. And often the suffix -*zake* is dropped in conversation.) **Those clouds within, the sediment, is made up of particles of rice that did not or could not ferment** and were permitted into the final product.

Long ago, all sake was *nigori*. Until perhaps a thousand years ago, **no one bothered to separate the completed sake from the rice particles** after fermentation. Records reveal a couple of different stories of what happened to change this.

One version is that a brewery in the erstwhile brewing capital of Itami, in modern-day Hyogo Prefecture, fired one its employees. The disgruntled and now jobless brewer snuck back into the *kura* and, as an act of vengeance, dumped copious amounts of

らも思い知るさ」と彼は考えたことだろう。

　そうとも、蔵人たちはたしかに思い知った。お酒を澄ませる方法を知ったのだ。木炭が米のかすを下に沈めたので、蔵人たちが何とかしようと網目の布で搾ったら、ほうら、どうだ！　透明なお酒ができたのだ。やがて、それが酒造りの標準になった。と、この話ではそうなっている。
　ところが、すぐ近くの奈良県で、もともと寺で酒造りをしていた僧たちが、酒「粕」を売っていたという記録がある。これは、米のかすを固めた白いもので、搾る工程、つまり網目の布で搾るときの副産物である。酒「粕」は、**漬物や、そのほか伝統的な食品に使用されるものだ。**

　奈良の僧たちがこれを売っていたという記録は、伊丹での木炭放り込み事件よりずっと前である。もし僧たちが「粕」を売っていたのなら、伊丹より前に酒を搾っていたことになる。
　とにかく、「にごり」を造りだしたのはだれかに関係なく、**今日のほとんどの酒は透明である。**
　「にごり酒」は「濾過していない酒」と呼ばれることがよくあるが、これはなかなかうまい言い方である。ただし完成した清酒はふつう、木炭の粉かセラミックのフィルターによる2度めの濾過工程も経ているので、米のかすを取り除く1度目の濾過は「上漕（しぼり）」と呼ばれることが多い。

powdered charcoal into a tank of just-completed, white sake. "That'll show 'em!" he likely thought.

Oh, it showed 'em all right. It showed them how to make clear sake. The charcoal dragged down the rice particles, and when the brewers pressed that through a mesh to try to save it, voila! They had clear sake, and that soon became the norm. Or so goes the story.

However, in nearby Nara Prefecture, there are records that show that the monks who primarily brewed in temples were selling sake *kasu*, the white cakes of rice particles that are the by-product of the pressing process, or passing the sake through a mesh. Sake *kasu* **is used in making pickles and in other traditional food**.

The monks in Nara have records of selling this stuff long before the charcoal-dumping event in Itami. If they were selling *kasu*, they had to have been pressing their sake before Itami.

Regardless of who started making *nigori*, **almost all sake today is clear**.

Nigorizake is often referred to as "unfiltered sake," and that is a perfectly good term. But because completed sake usually involves a second filtration process using either powdered charcoal or a ceramic filter, the first filtration that removes all the rice particles is often referred to as "pressing."

やがて、業界はほとんどの酒を搾るようになり、透明な酒が標準になった。ところが、田舎のほうでは**米農家の人たちが自分でお酒を造っていて**——もちろん違法だが——、わざわざ透明にしようとはしなかった。そこで1800年代後半に酒税法が改正されたとき、お酒は売る前に、網の目で濾さなければならないと決められた。その結果、**何十年もの間、「にごり酒」は市場の製品部門として存在しなかったのである。**

　かつて1966年のことだが、「月の桂」という銘柄を製造している、京都のとても有名な酒蔵が、「にごり」を斬新な製法で造ろうと思い立った。そして濁ったままで合法な「にごり」を造るため、酒税を監督している国税局に熱心に働きかけた。

　蔵元で社長の増田德兵衛は、当時のことをこう話している。「何ヵ月もかかりましたよ。一段階ごとに承認をもらわないといけなかったんです。何度もこう聞いたものです。『そこをこういうふうにしたら、認めてもらえますか、いかがですか？』、よかった、ではどうか承認してください、ってね」

　彼らは鳥かごのような装置を作った。それは穴のあいた挿入物で、酒のタンクにはめ込むようになっていた。穴から漏れて挿入物の中心へ集まった酒は、抜き取られて瓶詰めされる。政府は、網の目が直径2ミリメートル以下なら、かごを使って濾過したものも法的に日本酒とみなすと決定した。このときから、「にごり

In time, the industry moved toward pressing almost all sake, and clear sake became the norm. However, out in the countryside, **rice farmers would make their own sake**—illegally of course—and they would not bother to clarify it. So when the sake tax laws were rewritten in the late 1800s, it was stipulated that sake had to "pass through a mesh" before being sold. As a result, **for decades, *nigorizake* did not exist as a product genre on the market**.

Back in 1966 a very prominent brewery in Kyoto that produces the Tsuki no Katsura brand wanted to begin to make *nigori* in a new and better way. They worked very closely with the Ministry of Taxation, which oversees all these things, to create *nigori* that was legal but still cloudy.

Tokubee Masuda, the owner and president, explained that "it took several months, and at every step, we had to get their buy-in. We would ask, 'If we do it *this* way, it's acceptable, *right*?' Great, now sign off on it please."

What they did was create a cage-like device, an insert with holes in its walls that fit into a tank of sake. The sake that leaked through the holes into the center of the insert was then drawn off and bottled. The government determined that as long as the holes in the mesh were no larger than 2 millimeters

酒」はお酒の１つのジャンルとして誕生したのだ。ほかの酒蔵もやがて後に続き、それぞれの工夫を凝らした。「月の桂」は今、国内のどの「蔵」よりも多くの「にごり酒」を製造している。

　こうして「にごり」は、米のかすが残るように粗い網目で搾った酒を指すようになった。だが、どうしてこんなことをするのだろう？　それは、密造酒や1000年前の酒を彷彿とさせて楽しいからだ。

　わたしが酒蔵をいくつか訪れたとき、「にごり」の話題が出ると、杜氏たちがにんまりしながら声をひそめて、「にごり」を造るためにわざわざ**特別な粗い網目など使ったりしない**と教えてくれることがあった。
　「できあがった酒に酒粕を放り込むだけさ。もちろん違法だけどね……」

　脇に引っぱられて、こうささやかれたのは、わたしだけではなかったようだ。見たところ、どの杜氏もその方法で造っていたらしい。そして数年前、お酒を定義している肝心の法律の表現が変わっているのに気づいたのだ。以前は、上漕後、完成した酒に加えていいのは水だけだった。しかし今では、水と「粕」を加えることができる。どうやら**常識**と**実用性**が勝ったようだ——それとも、陳情運動の効果だろうか。

in diameter, the result of filtration using the cage could legally be considered sake. Hence, *nigorizake* was born as a genre of sake. Other breweries later followed suit, **using their own contraptions**. Tsuki no Katsura now makes more *nigorizake* than any *kura* in the country.

So *nigori* came to be sake that is pressed through a coarser mesh that allows some rice particles into the final product. Why is this done? Because it is a fun throwback to moonshine and the way sake was a millennium ago.

As I visited breweries and the topic of *nigori* came up, I would be told from time to time with a smile and in hushed tones that the brewer **did not bother to use a special, coarser mesh** to make *nigori*.

"We just throw some of the sake *kasu* back into it when we are done. But that is not totally legal, you see..."

Well, it seems that I was not the only one being pulled aside and whispered to. Apparently, everyone was doing it that way. And a few years ago, I noticed a change in the wording of the very laws that define sake. It used to be that after pressing, only water could be added to the completed sake. But now, water and *kasu* can be added. It seems that **common sense and practicality won out**—either that or effective lobbying.

「にごり酒」は海外で、とくにアメリカで人気がある（日本のほうがよっぽど人気がない）。どうしてだろう？　だれが造ろうと「にごり」と呼ぶからだと、推測する人もいる。また、だれが造ろうとその酒は白い。だから、覚えやすくて使いやすいのだ。

「にごり」はたしかに、とてもおいしいことがある。ふつうの酒より見るからに**濃厚で、ざらざらしていて、非常にとろみがある**。また、**かみごたえがあり、米の味がしてクリーミー**だ。だが、ふつうの酒のように上品ではなく、軽やかでもない。残っている米のかすのせいで、味と香りのほのかなニュアンスが消えてしまう。だが何事にも言えるように、これは好みの問題である。

こういう理由で、等級の高い「にごり」、たとえば「吟醸にごり」というのは、めったにない。等級の高さは、どれほど洗練されているかで決まる。かすを残すというのは正反対の方向だ。だから、実際「吟醸」クラスの「にごり」はわずかしかなく、ほとんどの「にごり」は等級が低い。

「うすにごり」という「にごり」、つまり「薄いにごり」があり、これは言葉どおりのもので、米のかすをほんの少しだけ残した「にごり酒」である。新鮮な味わいで、搾りたてのような魅力がある。この表示がある酒に「吟醸」クラスの高級酒がよくある。

「にごり」だからというだけで、どれも同じ味がする

Nigorizake is very popular outside of Japan, and in particular in the U.S. (It is much less popular in Japan.) Why might this be? Some surmise that it is because no matter who brews it, the sake is called *nigori*. And no matter who brews it, it is also white. So it is easy to remember and user friendly.

Nigori can be very enjoyable indeed. It is obviously **thicker and more textured, much more viscous** than regular sake, more **chewy, rice-like, and creamy**. However, it can never be as refined as regular sake, nor as light. The rice particles remaining will overpower any subtler nuances of flavor and aroma. As with all things, it is a matter of preference.

For this reason, rarely do we see higher grades of *nigori*, a "*ginjo nigori*," for example. Higher grades are all about increasing refinement. Leaving the dregs goes in the opposite direction. So, while there are in fact a few *nigori* of *ginjo* class out there, most *nigori* is of lower grades.

There are versions of *nigori* called *usu-nigori*, or "thin *nigori*," which is just what it sounds like: *nigorizake* in which only a very small amount of rice dust is allowed to remain. It has a kind of fresh, just-pressed appeal. Very often we see higher *ginjo* grades of sake in this manifestation.

Note also that just because a sake is a *nigori* **does**

わけではないことにも注意しよう。甘口の「にごり」、辛口の「にごり」、濃厚な「にごり」、薄い「にごり」だってある。なかには、かなりの量の米が浮いて見えるものもある。「生」の「にごり」もあるが、これは品質がとても変化しやすい。

　いずれにせよ、どれもが白く、「にごり」という名で呼ばれる。そして最後に、「にごり」はいつもおいしいのだ。

not mean it has to taste any one way. There is sweet *nigori*, dry *nigori*, thick *nigori*, and thin *nigori*. Some has visible chunks of rice suspended in it. There is even some *nigori* that is *nama*, although this can be quite unstable.

But it will always be white, and it will always be called *nigori*. In the end, it will always be enjoyable.

10. 特別酒

「特別本醸造酒」と「特別純米酒」という、ほかの名称の中に埋もれてしまっているような2つの名称の酒がある。たしかに一般にはあまり話題にならないが、日本酒通にとっては注目に値する酒である。

「特別」という言葉は、「ふつうと違う」という意味である。では、特別な「本醸造」と特別な「純米」について、何が特別なのか考えてみよう。

お酒の等級の図を見ると、この2つのクラスは「吟醸酒」と「純米吟醸酒」のすぐ下に、そして「本醸造酒」と「純米酒」のすぐ上に位置している。ひどいことに、これらを省略している片手落ちの図表もたくさんあるのだ！ だがこの2つの名称は**本物で、法的に定義された名誉ある名称**であり、どこかの酒蔵がつけたニックネームや用語などではない。ところが、お酒の統計学者（つまり政府）は、この名称のデータを、ふつうの「本醸造」やふつうの「純米酒」の統計値に含めてしまう傾向がある。政府でさえ、これらの名称を公平に扱っていないのだ！

では、実際の規則から始めよう。お酒に「特別本醸

10. *Tokubetsu*

There are two classifications of sake—*tokubetsu honjozo* and *tokubetsu junmai-shu*—that seem almost buried among the others. Certainly, they are less commonly mentioned, but they are very worthy of the sake connoisseur's attention.

The word *tokubetsu* means "special." Let's consider here just what is so special about special *honjozo* and special *junmai*.

If we look at a chart of sake grades, we see that these two classes sit just below *ginjo-shu* and *junmai ginjo-shu*, and just above *honjozo* and *junmai-shu*. On many less comprehensive charts they are egregiously omitted! But these two grades are **bona fide, legally defined grades of sake with full honors**, and not just nicknames or terms adopted by some brewers. Sake statisticians (read: the government), however, tend to embed data on these into their statistics on regular *honjozo* and regular *junmai-shu*. Even the government does not give these classifications their due!

Let us start with the actual rules. In order for a sake

造」や「特別純米」というラベルを貼るには、3つの条件のうち少なくとも1つを満たす必要がある。1つ目は、精米歩合が60％以下の米を使っていることだ。これはもちろん、「吟醸」クラスの資格をもっていることになる。2つ目は、「醸造好適米」、つまり適切な酒米で造られていることだ。ほとんどの高級酒が酒米で造られるのに対して、**安い酒はごくふつうの食用米で造られていることを覚えておこう**。3つ目──ここからが面白いのだが──、何かほかの理由で特別であり、その理由はラベルに書かれることになっている。

たしかに、これでは漠然としているように聞こえるだろう。地方の税務局の承諾があれば、さまざまな方法でお酒を「特別酒」にすることができるのだ。また、**その根拠をラベルに書くことになっている**が、わたしの経験では必ずしもそうではない。聞いたことのある具体的な例をひとつ挙げると、「大吟醸」を混ぜた「純米」というのがある。お酒に貼るラベルは、資格のある中でもっとも低い等級のものでなければならない。だが「大吟醸」を混ぜてあるなら、ラベルの名に恥じないほど特別なお酒だと言えるだろう。

とはいえ、約99％の場合、「特別酒」のラベルのある酒は、最初の2つの規則のどちらかに適合しているものだろう。言いかえれば、ほとんどの「特別本醸造」と「特別純米」は、「吟醸」レベルの精米歩合の米で造られているか、「醸造好適米」で造られているかのどちらかである。ほんの少しの例外もあるが、気にする必要

to be permitted to be labeled as *tokubetsu honjozo* or *tokubetsu junmai*, it must meet at least one of three requirements. One, it is made with rice milled down to 60 percent *seimai-buai* or further. This of course could qualify it as a *ginjo* class. Two, it is made using *shuzo koteki-mai*, or proper sake rice. Bear in mind that while almost all premium sake is made using sake rice, **most cheap sake is made using run-of-the-mill table rice**. Three—and here is where the fun starts—it is special for some other reason, which is supposed to be listed on the label.

In truth, this is as vague as it sounds. If approved by the local tax authorities, a number of methods can be used to make a sake *tokubetsu*. And while **the rationale is supposed to be explained on the label**, from my experience it not always is. The only concrete example I have ever heard of is a *junmai* that had some *daiginjo* mixed into it. Sake has to be labeled as the lowest grade for which it qualifies, but the mixed-in *daiginjo* made this particular sake special enough to qualify for the term on the label.

However, perhaps 99 percent of the time, a sake labeled as *tokubetsu* will have conformed to either of the first two rules. In other words, almost all *tokubetsu honjozo* and *tokubetsu junmai* are either made with rice milled to *ginjo* levels or made with *shuzo kotekimai*. There are only a few exceptions, and

はないだろう。

　個人的には、現行の「特別酒」の定義のための資格条件は、あまり重要でないと思う。根拠が精米歩合であれ、米であれ、またはほかのものであろうと、**酒蔵がこの酒をそのクラスだと決めたのなら、それで十分**である。たしかに書かれた仕様はすべて見るだろうが、味わってみる前に知る必要があるのは、その酒が酒蔵にとって「特別酒」であるということだけだ。実際、それ以上あっても気が散るだけだ。手元の酒について、せいぜい酒蔵の意図と感覚がわかったくらいで味わうほうがいい。

　それにしても、なぜ酒蔵は「特別酒」を造るのか？ たしかに、たとえば「純米」か「純米吟醸」と呼べるように微調整するほうが、「特別酒」という中間的な部門に置くより簡単ではないだろうか？　その答えは、**よくあるように販売促進のためである。**

　たとえば、ある酒蔵によく売れる「純米酒」があって、それも昔からあるとしよう。また、よく売れる「純米吟醸」もあって、これが主力商品であるとする。その酒蔵が、違う価格帯か、違う種類の商品を追加したいときに、もうひとつの「純米」や「純米吟醸」として発売したら、消費者には区別がつかないだろうし、今までの商品の売り上げが落ちるかもしれない。そこで、新商品を「特別純米」と名付けることによって、標準的な商品のどちらにも**影響が及ばないようにするの**

we need not worry about them.

Personally, I think the actual qualifying reason for the *tokubetsu* designation is of secondary importance. Whether due to the milling, the rice, or something else, it is enough for me to know **the brewer has ensconced this sake into that class**. I will certainly look at all available specs, but just knowing a sake was *tokubetsu* to the brewer is all I need to know before tasting it. In fact, anything beyond that would be distracting to me. I prefer to taste knowing little more than the brewer's intentions or feelings about the sake at hand.

Why in the world would a brewer make a *tokubetsu*? Surely it would be simpler to tweak a sake enough to call it either a *junmai* or a *junmai ginjo*, for example, rather than leave it in the limbo of the *tokubetsu* realm, would it not? The answer lies, **as many things do, in marketing**.

Let's say a sake brewer has a *junmai-shu* that sells well and has for a long time. And let's say that company has a *junmai ginjo* that also sells well and is perhaps a flagship product. When they want to add a product at a different price point or in a different style, adding another *junmai* or another *junmai ginjo* might be confusing to the market and even detract from the sales of the existing product. So by labeling it *tokubetsu junmai*, they **avoid encroaching on either**

である。

　これは、もちろん１つの例にすぎない。単純な動機もよくあって、新しくておもしろい酒ができたところ、おいしくてふつうの「純米酒」より明らかに品質が良いが、その酒蔵の「純米吟醸」の標準には及ばない場合などがそうだ。「特別純米」というのは、こういう酒にぴったりの名称である。

　驚くほどのことでもないが、この名称の代表となる酒は、かなり少数しか出回っていない。もっと本格的な「純米酒」・「純米吟醸」・「本醸造」・「吟醸」の方が、「特別純米」や「特別本醸造」よりもたくさんある。だがこれは、「特別」酒が注目に値しないと意味ではない。間違いなく注目に値する。

　それどころか、わたしにとっては、入手できる中でもっともおいしいお酒のいくつかが、この２つのあいまいな定義のクラスの中にあるのだ。ある酒蔵の「特別純米」が、また「特別本醸造」でさえ、長期間にわたってほかの製品よりきわめて飲みやすかったことが何度もある。

　時々、最高に楽しみたい特別な機会には、ふつうの「純米」や「本醸造」では少し平凡すぎることがある。また時には、「吟醸」酒がどの「吟醸」でも同じ味に感じることがあるだろう。これは当然で、酒蔵の個性を出すより、みな共通していることが「『吟醸』ブーム」の一因だと言えるのだ。だから「特別純米」や「特別本醸造」を飲むほうが、その酒蔵の特徴について多くを

one of their standard products.

This is of course just one example. The motivation often is as simple as coming out with something new and interesting that is delicious and clearly better than the average *junmai-shu* but not quite at the producer's standard for *junmai ginjo*. *Tokubetsu junmai* is **a perfect place for something like that.**

There are, not surprisingly, comparatively fewer representatives of these grades of sake out there. There are many more full-fledged *junmai-shu*, *junmai ginjo*, *honjozo*, and *ginjo* sake than *tokubetsu junmai* or *tokubetsu honjozo*. But that does not mean the *tokubetsu* sake do not warrant our attention. They most certainly do.

In fact, to me, these two tenuously defined classes offer some of the most enjoyable sake available. On some occasions I have found the *tokubetsu junmai* or even *tokubetsu honjozo* products of a brewer to be eminently more drinkable over the long term than any other product.

Sometimes, regular *junmai-shu* and *honjozo* are almost a smidgen too plebeian for maximum enjoyment. And, once in a while, a *ginjo* sake will taste more like every other *ginjo* out there. As good as that can be, it can seem to be a part of the "*ginjo* borg" collective rather than display the brewer's individuality. So **I can occasionally learn much more**

学べることがある。たしかに「大吟醸」のほうが良い酒かもしれないが（基準に従えば）、表面上は等級の低いこれらの酒を飲むことで、その酒蔵や杜氏のことや、彼らの意図がよくわかるのである。

しかし定義があいまいなので、2つの「特別酒」は、「吟醸」のような繊細さを出すこともあれば、低い精米歩合の米を使うことで、さまざまなこくを持っていることもある。その結果すばらしいバランスが生まれたりする。だから「特別酒」は、わたしにとって一番お気に入りの酒のひとつなのだ。

about a brewer's style by drinking their *tokubetsu junmai* or *tokubetsu honjozo*. Sure, their *daiginjo* might be better sake (according to some standards), but I see more of the brewery, the brewer, and their intentions by drinking these ostensibly lower grades.

However vaguely defined, the two *tokubetsu* classes can exude some of the finer appeal of *ginjo* while maintaining the fuller arrays of richer flavors possible with less highly milled rice. The result can be an exquisite balance. This is why the *tokubetsu* are some of my favorite sake.

11. 「山廃」と「生酛」

「山廃仕込み」と「生酛仕込み」で造られるお酒は、一般に入手しやすくなり、興味を持たれるようになってきていて、この流行はこれからも続きそうだ。それにもかかわらず、「山廃」と「生酛」についての簡潔ですぐれた説明を見つけるのは難しい。その意義についてはなおさらである。でもまあ、安心してほしい。ここですべて明らかにされるから。

これらが何なのか、またなぜそうするのかを説明するには、数百年前にさかのぼらねばならない。その頃も今と同じように、**お酒は酒母（酛）造りから始まった**。米、「麹」、水を、腰ほどの高さの小さな桶に入れる。これを専用の棒ですりつぶしてピューレ状にする。これは力のいる作業で、しかも何時間も同じことを繰り返さなければならない。あまりにも退屈なので、ひまつぶしと眠気覚ましと、そして数を忘れないために、**杜氏たちは伝統的な歌をいくつか作ったものだ**。

これが、12世紀の酒造りの始めから20世紀初頭まで、ほぼ唯一の酒母の造り方であり、「生酛」という名で知られるようになった。その後の1900年代前半に、日本酒研究家たちが、**大変なすりつぶしの作業は必**

11. *Yamahai* and *Kimoto* Sake

Sake made using the *yamahai-shikomi* method or the *kimoto* method are **becoming more commonly available and attracting more interest**, and this trend will likely continue. Nevertheless, it is hard to find a good, concise explanation of *yamahai* and *kimoto*, much less of their significance. But relax, your search ends here.

To explain what they are and why they are, we need to go back several hundred years. Then, as now, a tank of **sake began with a batch of yeast starter (*moto*)**. Rice, *koji*, and water were all put into a small, waist-high tank. This was then mixed into a puree-like consistency using poles adapted to this purpose. This was rough work and took many hours of repetitive labor to accomplish. It was so tedious that **the brewers developed traditional songs** to help pass the time, keep awake, and not lose count.

This was for the most part the only method of creating the yeast starter from its inception in the 12th century until the early 20th century, and it came to be known as *kimoto*. Then, in the early 1900s, sake

しも**必要ないこと**を発見した。杜氏たちは水の量や温度を調節しながら粘り強く試して、ついに大変な作業なしで同じ結果を生み出せるようになった。この方法は、棒での作業以外はあらゆる点で本来の「生酛」とほぼ同類であり、「山廃」という名で呼ばれた。この言葉は、**棒ですりつぶす作業の廃止**を意味していて、これが2つの方法のおもな違いである。つまり、「生酛」は**退屈なすりつぶし作業が必要**であり、「山廃」では行われないのだ。

ここでちょっと脱線して、化学的に何が起こっているのか見てみよう。この章では説明しきれない化学変化がいくつか起こった後、乳酸菌が空気中からタンクに入る。これが増殖し、当然多くの乳酸を作る。そして今度は乳酸がほかの雑菌と悪い酵母を殺し、**最後には自分を産んだ乳酸菌も殺してしまう**。我々にとって非常にありがたい自然の驚異のおかげで、**清酒酵母が好む環境**となり、ここなら酵母は自力で生き抜くことができるのだ。そこで酵母が投入されて増殖し、健康な酒母となり、やがて健康な発酵へと導いていく。

空気中の野生酵母が化学的要因によって中に入るかもしれないが、今日ではほとんどの酒が、自然淘汰されないよう厳選した酵母を加えて造られている。

researchers discovered that **all that hard mixing work was not really necessary**. By adjusting water volume, temperature, and doses of patience, brewers could achieve the same result without the exertion. This method, closely related to the original *kimoto* method in all ways save the physical pole manipulation, took the name *yamahai*. The meaning of this word conveys **the cessation of pole pushing**, and this is the main difference between the two methods: *kimoto* **calls for the tedious mixing with poles**, while this is not done in the *yamahai* method.

Let us go off on a tangent for a moment and look at what happens chemically. After a few chemical processes that are beyond the scope of this chapter take place, lactic bacteria fall into the tank from the air. These guys proliferate, and as they do they create lots of lactic acid. This in turn **kills other bad bacteria and undesirable yeast and eventually kills the lactic bacteria that begot it**. By some miracle of nature for which we should all feel immense gratitude, **sake yeast actually like this environment**, and they alone can survive in it. So they drop in and proliferate, leading to a healthy yeast starter and eventually a healthy fermentation.

Naturally occurring sake yeast cells floating in the air will drop in when the chemistry invites them; however, today, almost all sake is made by adding

「山廃」が開発されて、お酒の醸造技術が大きく飛躍したとき、研究者たちは、それが乳酸によるものだと気づいた。「どうして乳酸菌が乳酸を作るのを待つ必要があるんだ？　自分たちで入れたらいいじゃないか」と彼らは考えた。そこでやってみたのが、「速醸酛(そくじょうもと)」の名で知られる方法の始まりである。「速醸」という言葉は「速い醸造」を示す。だが酒瓶のラベルに載っていることはほとんどない。**「速醸酛」は既定の醸造方法**になり、存在する酒の99％以上で使用されているからだ。

　ここで振り返ってみよう。「山廃」と「生酛」は古く伝統的な方法で、どちらも乳酸菌を利用して乳酸を作り、環境を浄化して清酒酵母のための準備をする。一方「速醸酛」は、**化学実験室から乳酸を持ってきて、すぐに加える**。

　注意してほしいのは、「山廃」や「生酛」が、自然発生の酵母を意味しているのではないということだ。自然発生の乳酸菌である。誤解しないように！　非常にまれだが、自然発生の酵母も使用される。ほんの一握りの酒蔵がそのリスクを負って造っている。だが、その方法で酒を造る場合、絶対に「生酛」か「山廃」でなければならず、そうでないと決してうまくいかない。
　こららの製法には実際、それぞれ認められた長所が

carefully selected yeast rather than leaving it to natural selection.

The evolution of sake brewing took a giant leap forward when, just after the *yamahai* method was developed, researchers realized it was all about lactic acid. "Why do we need to wait for the bacteria to create it for us when we can just add it ourselves?" they thought. And so they did, giving rise to the process known as *sokujo-moto*. The word *sokujo* suggests "fast-brew"; the term is almost never seen on the bottle, however, as **sokujo-moto has become the default brewing method**, used in over 99 percent of all sake in existence.

To review: *yamahai* and *kimoto* are older, traditional methods that both utilize natural lactic bacteria to produce lactic acid, which then cleans out the environment in preparation for the sake yeast cells. *Sokujo-moto* **gets lactic acid from the chemistry lab and adds it straightaway**.

Note, *yamahai* and *kimoto* do *not* imply naturally occurring yeast; they imply naturally occurring lactic bacteria. Beware this misperception! Very, very rarely is naturally occurring yeast used. Just a handful of brewers take that risk. But when they do make sake that way, it absolutely must be either *kimoto* or *yamahai*, or it simply will not work.

There are real and perceived advantages to these

ある。「山廃」と「生酛」の方法は、酵母を加える前の化学変化を終えるのに約2週間かかる。だが「速醸」はこの2週間を省けるので、製造時間を大幅に短縮できる。「速醸」の味も一般に軽やかで、あっさりしており、それが消費者にとって魅力となっている（人によって違うので、魅力となるよう造られている、としておこう）。

「山廃」と「生酛」の醸造では、2週間余分にかかるので、酒母を造るのに合計1ヵ月かかる。でもこの2つの方法により、こくと、旨味と、奥深さのある酒が生まれるのだ。また、酸味があり、甘く、匂いが強い。

「杜氏（醸造者）」が、この2つのどちらかを用いるのには、技術的な理由がある。「山廃」は「生酛」より力強い味になる傾向があって、甘さと匂いがきつくなることが多く、反対に「生酛」はほのかに酸味があり、きめの細かい味がする。「山廃」も「生酛」も、「速醸」に比べると、全体的にこくがあり旨味が多いのが特徴である。

「山廃」はとくに、また「生酛」もある程度、必ずしもそれほど野性的で匂いがきついわけではない。なかには力強いほど野性的なものもあって、甘味と酸味が互いにバランスを取りながらも強烈な味わいを持っているものがある。だが多くの「山廃」と「生酛」では、匂いがきつすぎることはめったにない。ラベルに「山

methods. It takes about two weeks for the *yamahai* and *kimoto* methods to do their chemical thing before the yeast can be added. But *sokujo* cuts those two weeks out, shortening the production time significantly. The flavor of *sokujo* is also generally **lighter and simpler**, which appeals to (or has been made to appeal to, depending on whom you talk to) consumers.

The additional two weeks in *yamahai* and *kimoto* brewing means a total of one month just to create the yeast starter. But these two methods produce sake with more richness, umami, and depth. They can also be tarter, sweeter, and gamier.

There are technical reasons a *toji* (brewer) may use one of these two methods. *Yamahai* tends to be **more intense** than *kimoto*, often showing **more sweetness and gaminess** as opposed to **the subtle tartness and fine-grained quality to the flavor** of many *kimoto*. Both *yamahai* and *kimoto* share some of the rich, umami-laden aspects when collectively compared to *sokujo*.

Yamahai in particular and *kimoto* to a degree are not always so wild and gamey. There are some that are powerfully so, with sweetness and acidity that may balance each other well but are nonetheless intense. However, there are many *yamahai* and *kimoto* that are barely noticeably gamey. Do not do

廃」や「生酛」とある酒は口に合わないと決めつけるような、ひどいことはしないでほしい。ほのかにこくがあるだけで、大して違わないこともあるのだ。実際、消費者に誤解されたくないために、ラベルに「山廃」と書かない酒蔵もある。この2つの製法で造られた酒は、野性的な味になる傾向があるが、じつは「山廃」と「生酛」にはさまざまな味があるのだ。どうか、**先入観は捨ててほしい！**

　これらの方法は、お酒のさまざまな等級とは無関係である。「普通酒」から「大吟醸」まで、どの酒でも「山廃」や「生酛」、または「速醸」でありうる。たとえば「山廃」のこくは「大吟醸」の軽やかさとは矛盾するようだが、その組み合わせは本当にある。もちろん、ふつうの「純米山廃」のほうが一般的ではある。

　では、ここで覚えてほしいのは次のことだ。「山廃」と「生酛」はともに自然の乳酸菌を使用し（自然発生の酵母ではない！）、造るのに2週間長くかかり、野性的で強烈な味わいを持つことが多い。「山廃」は、本来の方法の「生酛」で行う、棒でのすりつぶしを省き、たいてい匂いがきつくなる。「速醸」は簡単で清潔で、旨味は少ないものの、半分の時間で酒母が完成する。

　どの方法が優れているということはない。自分で好みを見つけるまでは。

yourself the disservice of assuming that a sake with *yamahai* or *kimoto* printed on the label is going to be a whack on your palate. It may be subtly richer, or not even noticeably different. In fact, some brewers avoid writing *yamahai* on the label for fear of inviting misperceptions from consumers. While sake made by one of these two methods tend to be wilder, there is in truth a range of flavors and styles to *yamahai* and *kimoto*. **Just avoid prejudice!**

These methods have nothing to do with the various grades of sake. Anything from a *futsu-shu* to a *daiginjo* can be a *yamahai*, *kimoto*, or *sokujo*. *Yamahai* richness may contradict the lightness of *daiginjo*, for example, but that combination does indeed exist, even if regular *junmai yamahai* are more common.

So the take-home here is that *yamahai* and *kimoto* share the use of natural lactic bacteria (*not* naturally occurring yeast!), take two weeks longer to make, and often taste wilder and more intense. *Yamahai* eschews the pole-mixing used in the original method of *kimoto* and is usually the gamier of the two. *Sokujo* is simpler and cleaner, albeit with less umami, and is completed in half the time.

No one style is better than another. Not until, that is, you find your own preferences.

12. 地域性

　日本はカリフォルニア州より少し面積が小さく、北東から南西に、ざっと800マイルにわたって伸びている。現在、お酒は47都道府県のどの県でも造られている。(2、3の県は、ほんのしるし程度の量を造っているだけで、最近まで製造していなかった)。

　どの県にも、それぞれの地形と天候がある。だが、お酒にもワインのような地域性があるのだろうか？ つまり、日本のある地域でできた酒は、その地に関係する特徴を持っているだろうか？ そしてほかの地域でできた酒は、産地を特定できるような違う性質を持っているだろうか？

　端的に答えると、そう、その通りである。そして、お酒の地域性を学ぶのはとてもおもしろいのだ。ところが、それはまったく漠然としており、ワインの世界のように**明白に表されていないし、産地を特定できるものでもない**。地域の特徴を反映している県もあれば、まったく個性のない県もある。個性のない地域の酒がおいしくないという意味ではない。それどころか、お酒で有名ではない地方のものが抜群であったりする。だが全般的に日本の約60％の地域には、その地に関

12. Regionality

Japan is a bit smaller than California and runs about eight hundred miles roughly northeast to southwest. Today sake is made in every single one of its forty-seven prefectures. (A couple prefectures just make a token amount and did not make any sake at all until recently.)

Each prefecture has its own terrain and climate. But does sake, like much wine, have regionality? That is, does sake from one part of Japan have a style or profile that can be associated with it, and sake from another region a different but just as identifiable nature?

The short answer is yes, it does, and regionality in sake is extremely interesting to study. However, it is **decidedly vaguer** and not as **clearly delineated or identifiable** as it is in the wine world. Some prefectures reflect regional distinctions and some do not have much individuality at all. This does not mean that the sake from those nondescript regions are not good. On the contrary, sake from some regions not known for their sake can be outstanding. But overall,

係する特徴を持つ酒が、少なくともいくつかはある。

　そう、だから、**お酒には地域性がある**のだ。

　さらに、そういう特徴のある地域でも、「蔵」が全部その特徴どおり造るとは限らない。故意にせよ、そうでないにせよ、反対する「蔵」があるものだ。しかし、特徴のある地域の約60〜70％の「蔵」が、産地を特定できるような酒を造っている。これもまた、合格点として十分だろう。

　数多くの要因が、それぞれの地域の特徴に影響を与えている。第一に、天候がある。**産地の温度は、お酒の味にとてつもなく影響する**。日本の北部はもちろん、南部よりかなり気温が低い。日本の北東部で造られる酒は、南西部の酒よりも低い温度で醸造され、やがて熟成される。醸造温度と熟成温度が低いと、一般に軽やかですっきりした酒になる。温度が温かいと、豊かな幅広い味になる。どちらが本質的に優れているということはない。それは単に好みの問題だ。

　産地がお酒の特徴に影響を与えるもう１つの要因は、料理である。ずっと昔、地域による特徴が表れた頃、山に住む人々は新鮮な刺身を毎日食べることはできなかった。寒くてじめじめした地方での食事はほとんどが保存食で、こってりしたもの、甘いもの、塩辛

perhaps 60 percent of the regions of Japan have at least some style of sake associated with them.

So yes, **sake has regionality**.

Furthermore, in any region that does have an associated regional style, not all the *kura* in the region conform to that style. You'll always have dissenters, deliberately or otherwise. But in any given region that has a style, perhaps 60 to 70 percent of the *kura* in that area will brew sake in that identifiable style. Again, that is enough for a passing grade.

A number of factors have contributed to the sake style of each region. First there is climate. **The temperature of a region affects the flavors of sake immensely**. The northern regions of Japan are of course much colder than those in the south. Sake made in the northeast part of Japan is both fermented and subsequently matured at lower temperatures than sake made in the southwest part of Japan. Colder fermentation and storage temperatures generally lead to lighter, cleaner sake. Warmer temperatures lead to fuller, broader flavors. Neither is intrinsically better than the other; it is simply a matter of preference.

Another factor that affects the style of sake from a given region is cuisine. Long ago when regional styles came into being, people in the mountains did not have a daily diet of fresh sashimi. Most of what they had in those cold, damp regions was preserved

いものが多かった。当然のことながら、そのような食事のまわりで造られる酒は、料理の味を引き立てるように甘くてこってりしたものだった。

これと、大きな漁港のある町を比べてみよう。港町では昔、小作農でさえ釣れるたびに新鮮な魚を食べていた。こういう場所で造られる酒は、その地で食べる料理がある程度影響して、軽やかでやわらかな味になった。

日本各地で育つ米も、お酒の特徴の一因となった。少なくとも、米がいろんな場所へ運べるようになるまではそうだった。西日本の米は北部の米より粒が大きく、温かな気温と相まって、寒い気候の小さな粒のものよりも大らかな味がする。水も要因となっているが、その役割はあまり重要ではない。**水はその地域全体で、必ずしも一定の品質ではないからだ。**水はある酒蔵では酒の特徴に影響しているかもしれないが、産地と水を関連付けるのが難しい顕著な例外がいくつかあるのだ。

お酒の特徴に影響している、もう1つの伝統的な要因は、**各地を取り仕切っていた杜氏組合（醸造者の組合）**である。この男たちは（昔は男ばかりだった）、夏は自分の土地を耕し、秋には近づく酒造りの時期のために近隣の酒蔵へやってくる。そして春になると、杜氏たちは家へ戻り、農作業の合間に皆で酒を飲んで意見を交わす。やがて彼らは、酒造りの工程を助けあい

food, often heavy, sweet, and salty. Naturally enough, the sake that developed around food like that was sweeter and heavier, so as to complement it.

Contrast this with towns near big fishing ports, where long ago even the peasants were enjoying fresh fish as often as they could catch it. The sake brewed near these places was much lighter and softer due in part to what the people there ate.

The rice that grew in each part of Japan also contributed to sake styles, at least before rice could be practically shipped to here and there. The rice that grows in the west is larger than that which grows up north, and along with the warmer temperatures, this leads to bigger flavors than its cold-weather, smaller-grain counterparts. Water plays its part too, although its role is more tenuous because **water is not necessarily consistent across any given region**. Water may affect the style of sake in any one given brewery, but with a few notable exceptions it is hard to link region and water.

One more factor that traditionally affected sake styles is **the guilds of *toji* (brewers) that were dominant in each region**. These guys (and guys they were, back in the day) would farm their own land in the summer and travel to nearby breweries in the fall for the upcoming brewing season. Come spring, the *toji* would return home, and between farming chores

促進するための系統だった組織を作った。これは、さまざまな杜氏組合が、酒造りについてそれぞれ**固有の方法や秘訣を持って**いたことを意味している。そのほとんどは、地元の天候のもとで、地元の米を使い、地元の酒蔵で得られた経験から生まれたのである。

その後それぞれの杜氏組合が、自分たちの酒に際立った特徴を与える方法を開発した。「あそこの酒は本物の南部杜氏風だ」とか、「あの男は本当の丹波杜氏のやり方で造っていないぞ」とか──、こういう類の意見を、酒にのめりこんでいる人がつぶやいているのが聞こえることがある(そして、たまたまそばに立っていた、わたしのような人間の耳に入るのだ)。

皮肉なことに、お酒の地域性のもとになっている同じ要因が、今日では、**地域による違いを台なし**にする原因になっていることもある。

料理について考えてみよう。今日、海から遠く離れた山の人々も、自転車でコンビニへ行けば、毎日のように新鮮な刺身を食べることができる。また、海沿いで新鮮な魚を食べている人々だって、ステーキを食べたい夜があるかもしれない。いろいろな食品が入手できるようになり、**地元の料理には制限がなくなった**ので、お酒の地域的な特徴への必要性も変化してきたのだ。

慣例からの脱却も、伝統的な「杜氏」制度に変化を

they would drink together and exchange notes. Eventually they created structured organizations to aid, assist, and promote their brewing prowess. What this means is that the various guilds all had **their own methods and tricks of the trade**. Most of these were born of experience gained in local breweries, using local rice in local climates.

The various guilds then developed methods that led to noticeable characteristics in their final sake. "Their sake is a true Nanbu guild style," or "That guy is not really brewing in a true Tanba Toji manner"—these kinds of comments can still be heard muttered by those who are deep enough into it (and overheard by people like me who just happen to be standing near them).

Ironically, some of these same factors that have contributed to regionality in sake are today also partly responsible for the **undoing of regional distinctions**.

Consider cuisine. These days, people in the mountains far from the sea can enjoy fresh sashimi on a daily basis with a bicycle ride to the local convenience store. And the fresh-fish folks down by the ocean might prefer steak some nights. As availability of certain foods blossoms and **local cuisine loses its grip**, the need for a particular local style of sake changes as well.

Another break from custom is a change in the

もたらしている。その昔、「蔵」は必ずもっとも近い組合から「杜氏」を雇ったものだったが、今日では「杜氏」はどこからでも来てもらえる。また、「蔵」はどの組合の「杜氏」も雇わずに、自分たちだけで酒造りすることもできる。醸造技術も方法も今では広く入手できるので、酒蔵は、かつての地元特有の酒とは違う特徴や製法を採用できるのだ。

地域の特徴を保つための法律はないし、使用できる原料や製法を命じる法律もない。酒蔵は好きなように酒を造ることができる。地元の酒に使う米は、国内のどこから運んできてもかまわない。ほとんどの「蔵」は地元の米を少なくともいくらかは使おうとしているし、地元の米だけを大量に使う「蔵」も少しはある（よし、えらいぞ！）。だが、多くは最高の「大吟醸」のために兵庫県の山田錦を求める。お酒そのものについても同様で、地元の酒は**地域性**という**弱点**があるからと、わざわざ遠くの米を使用するのだ。

その上、はっきりした特徴のある1つの県の中でも、決まって一握りの「蔵」がその特徴に合わせようとしないものだ。そういう「蔵」は、ほかの影響を受けてきたのかもしれない。特殊な杜氏がいたとか、前の蔵元が酒の味について独自の考えを持っていたとかだろう。もしくは、酒蔵の集団から自分たちを区別させたいだけかもしれない。いずれにせよ、地元の規範と違う酒を造る酒蔵は、常にあるだろう。

traditional *toji* system. Long ago, a *kura* would almost certainly employ a *toji* from the closest guild, but today a *toji* can come from just about anywhere. A *kura* might even brew by themselves, without a *toji* from any guild. Brewing technologies and methods are more widely accessible now, so a brewery may employ methods or styles that are different from what would lead to the erstwhile local style of sake.

Nor are there any laws to keep regional styles in place or to dictate what raw materials or methods can be used. Brewers are free to make sake any way they please. The rice used in a local brew can come from anywhere in Japan. Most *kura* try to use at least some local rice, and a few make a big deal of using *only* local rice (good on them!). But many insist upon Yamada Nishiki from Hyogo for their top *daiginjo*, and as good as this is for the sake itself, using rice from far away for your local sake is **a chink in the armor of regionality**.

Furthermore, within any one prefecture that does in fact have a clear style, inevitably a handful of *kura* will not be consistent with that style. They may have had other influences, like one particular *toji* or a former owner who had his own ideas of how sake should taste. Or perhaps they just want to differentiate themselves from the pack. But there will always be some that make sake that is different from

現代の市場状況も、酒蔵が取り組まねばならないもう1つの現実である。**欲しいお酒がどこからでも翌日に玄関に届く**という、今日の驚異的なインフラが意味することは、今や蔵元たちは地元の田舎者だけではなく、もっと大きな市場に向けて酒を造っているということだ。そのように、世界中とは言わないまでも、大都市の人々を惹きつける酒を造る必要があるのだ。そういう酒はたしかにおいしいだろうが、**特徴という点では均一化されてくる**。ある地域の「吟醸」がその地ならではの特徴を持つというよりも、どこの「吟醸」も同じような味になりつつある。小規模の酒蔵の多くは、「普通酒」の市場を経済規模の大きい大企業に奪われてしまったので、均質化された「吟醸」や高級酒をたくさん作るようになってきている。これは悪いことではない――ただ、地域による独自の特徴が変化していることを意味しているのだ。

　こうして地域性を与えたり減じたりしているすべての要因が、同時に、あいまいだが興味深い状況を作っている。それでも、**お酒の地域性に適用できる、大ざっぱだが役に立つ法則**があるのだ。それは吟味に耐え、業界の専門家によって認められてもいる（つまり、わたしがでっち上げたのではない！）

　北東の方へ行くほど、お酒はきめ細かく、**引き締**

the local norm.

Modern market conditions are another reality with which brewers must contend. The amazing infrastructure that, today, **lets me get any sake I want from any part of the country delivered to my door the next day** means brewers now make sake for markets much bigger than just the local yokels. As such they need to make sake that appeals to people in the big cities, if not all over the world. Even if such sake is undoubtedly tasty, it does **become homogenized in terms of style**. The *ginjo* of a given region tends to taste like the *ginjo* of all regions, rather than the original style of sake from that area. With many smaller brewers seeing their market for *futsu-shu* dry up as they lose it to larger companies with better economies of scale, more production goes toward such homogenized *ginjo* and premium sake. This is not a bad thing—but it often means a shift from original regional styles.

Having contributing and detracting factors all in play at the same time leads to a very vague but interesting state of affairs. There is, however, **a general but useful rule that can be applied to sake regionality**, one that stands up to scrutiny and is echoed by experts in the industry (meaning: I didn't just make this up!).

The farther northeast you go, **the more**

まった味になる。軽やかで繊細で辛口であることが多いが、必ずというわけではない。一般には、多くの味が狭いところにぎゅっと詰め込まれたような、こぢんまりした味である。逆に西の方へ行くほど、**骨太で、こくがあり、広がりのある**味になる。西日本の酒はこってりして甘いものが多い。

これは、上述したすべての要因、つまり天候、米、「杜氏」組合、その他によるものだ。明らかに大ざっぱな概括だが、使えるものである。

北東から南西へと、きめ細かい酒から骨太の酒へ徐々に変化していく一方で、例外もある。しかもたくさんだ。県全体で独自の特徴を持っているところもあれば、すばらしい酒を造っているのに、はっきりした特徴のない県もある。それでも、この法則は半分以上当てはまるので、参考にしていいだろう。

特徴のはっきりした**地域の例**として、覚えやすいものがいくつかある。新潟は、明らかにもっとも独特な特徴を持つところだ。辛口で、軽やかで、素朴な味である。「淡麗辛口」という名がつけられ、県のほとんど100％という高い割合の酒蔵がこの銘柄を造っている。その次は兵庫県の灘だろう。国内で最大の酒どころであり、辛口で、こくがあり、決して派手ではない酒を造っている。比較的近くにあるのが京都の伏見で、甘い水のおかげで、やさしく繊細な、いくらか甘口の酒になり、京都の上品な料理に非常によく合う。

fine-grained and compact the sake gets. It is often light, delicate, and dry, but not always. It is commonly tight, as if a lot of flavor got compacted into a narrow girth. And conversely, the farther west you go, **the more big-boned, rich, and broad** the sake flavors get; more sake in this part of Japan are heavier and sweet.

This is due to everything presented above: climate, rice, *toji* guilds, and more. And while this is admittedly a big generalization, it's a workable one.

Along this northeast-southwest continuum of fine-grained to big-boned sake, there are exceptions. Plenty of 'em. There are entire prefectures that are doing their own thing style-wise, and others that have no clear style, great stuff though their sake may be. Still, this rule applies more than half the time, which means we can use it as a reference.

There are a handful of easily remembered **examples of regions with a clear style**. Niigata is easily the place with the most identifiable style: dry, light, and pristine. *Tanrei-karakuchi* is the term they have adopted, and an extremely high percentage of the almost one hundred breweries in the prefecture fit this description well. Next would likely be the Nada region in Hyogo Prefecture, the largest brewing region in the country, which has dry, rich sake that is decidedly not ostentatious. Comparatively close by is the Fushimi region of Kyoto, whose soft water leads

広島には、ほとんどの地域で甘い水があり、やわらかくて甘口の酒ができる。だが一方、四国の高知の酒は辛口でがっしりした味であり、これは1人あたりの飲酒量が平均よりはるかに高いという文化によるものだ。山形は、ほかの県より高い割合で「吟醸」を造っているので、ここの酒の多くは軽やかでフルーティーである。

　福島は海岸と平野と山に恵まれているので、お酒の特徴もほかの地域に比べて幅広い種類があり、この県全体の特徴を決めるのは難しい。ここについては、とくに話しておきたい。福島は、2011年3月11日に発生した大地震と原発事故に遭った県のひとつだからだ。その時までに酒造りのシーズンは終わっており、田んぼにも米はなかった。2、3の「蔵」だけが核施設に近かったので、避難しなければならなかった。だが、ほかの酒蔵はすべて遠く離れていて、厚い壁と密閉された建物で守られており、おかげで酒は無事だったのだ。

　福島の日本酒業界は、世間の不安に対して効果的で説得力のある対応をしてきた。あらゆる外観や材料が何度もチェックされる。お酒になる米、醸造に使う水、そして完成品もすべて、第三者機関によってテストさ

to gentle, delicate, and somewhat sweet sake that goes decidedly well with the refined cuisine of Kyoto.

Hiroshima, or most of it anyway, has soft water that contributes to soft and sweet sake, whereas Kochi on the island of Shikoku has extremely dry sake with a solid structure that is a result of its culture of drinking significantly more per capita than the average region. Yamagata makes a higher ratio of *ginjo* than any other prefecture, so much of the sake from there is light and fruity.

Fukushima is blessed with ocean coast, plains, and mountains, giving it a wider range of sake types than most places and making it hard to assign an overall style to sake from that prefecture. It deserves special mention because it is one of several prefectures affected by the massive earthquake and nuclear accident that occurred on March 11, 2011. By that time the sake-brewing season was wrapping up, and there was no rice in the ground. Only a couple of *kura* were so close to the nuclear reactor that they had to evacuate the area. All the other breweries in the region were far enough away and protected with thick-walled, sealed buildings that kept the sake safe.

The Fukushima sake industry has responded to public concern in effective and convincing ways. Every aspect and ingredient is checked several times. The rice that goes into the sake, the water used in

れている。福島産の酒は1本残らずテストされ、許容範囲を超えるセシウムやその他の有害物質が見つかったものは1滴もない。

　ここで挙げた地域の特徴は、ほんの少しの例である。この話題は全体的に少々漠然としたものだし、解釈は自由なので、すべての地域をどう比べるかについて、きっとさまざまな意見があることだろう。

　わたしにとってお酒でもっとも楽しいことのひとつは、**少なくとも基本的な地域性を理解**してから、それぞれの酒を味わってみて、その地域についての自分の知識と比べてみることだ。**行き当たりばったりの練習**だが、それでもやはり、いつやっても面白いのである。

brewing, and the final product are all tested by a third party. Every single bottle of sake from Fukushima is tested and not a single drop has been found to have a higher-than-permissible level of cesium or other adverse elements.

The regional styles discussed here are but a few examples, and because this whole subject is a bit vague and open to interpretation there will certainly be various opinions as to how all the regions compare.

To me one of the most enjoyable aspects of sake is **getting at least a basic grip on sake regionality** and then comparing the taste of each sake to what I think I know about its region. This can be **a bit of a hit or miss exercise**, but it is is nevertheless always an interesting one.

Index
索引

Index 索引

A

aged sake *43, 47, 81, 83, 85, 87, 89, 91*

aroma *17, 29, 41, 47, 49, 57, 61, 77, 97, 159*

aromatic *21, 49, 57, 63, 69, 71, 97, 107, 109, 133, 139*

aru-ten *59, 61, 63, 65*

Aspergillus oryzae *19, 117*

atsukan *145*

B·C

brewed beverage *17*

brewery *123, 151, 155, 157, 171, 187, 189, 191, 195, 197*

brewing year *89*

BY *88, 89, 90, 91*

choki-jukuseishu *43, 89*

D·E

daiginjo *35, 37, 39, 41, 59, 61, 87, 107, 109, 113, 117, 133, 165, 171, 181, 191*

distilled alcohol *36, 39, 41, 55, 61, 117*

distilled beverage *17*

enzyme *17, 19*

F

fermentable materials *17, 117*

fermentation *17, 19, 33, 41, 57, 151, 175, 185*

flavor *17, 29, 41, 43, 47, 49, 51, 57, 61, 71, 87, 89, 121, 131, 143, 159, 171, 179, 181, 185, 187, 195*

flavoring *121*

fruit-flavored *121*

futsu-shu *37, 39, 41, 55, 57, 59, 111, 117, 119, 121, 125, 181, 193*

G

genshu *36, 43*

ginjo *21, 25, 35, 36, 37, 39, 41, 47, 49, 59, 61, 97, 105, 107, 109, 111, 117, 137, 139, 141, 143, 147, 159, 163, 165, 171, 193, 197*

ginjo nigori *159*

Ginjo, schminjo *109, 111, 113, 141*

gluten *115, 117, 119, 121, 125*

gonjo nigori *159*

grade of sake *35, 36, 55, 57, 59, 107, 159, 163, 169, 181*

H

hiochi *77*

hiya-oroshi *73*

hon-nama *75*

honjozo 35, 36, 41, 59, 109, 111, 117, 163, 169

hot versus cold 137

husk 19

J

junmai 35, 36, 39, 41, 55, 57, 59, 61, 63, 65, 87, 107, 109, 117, 119, 123, 125, 133, 163, 165, 167, 169

junmai daiginjo 35, 37, 39, 59, 65, 107, 123

junmai ginjo 35, 37, 39, 59, 65, 107, 123, 163, 167, 169

junmai yamahai 180

K

kanzake 145

kijoshu 43

kimoto 43, 145, 173, 175, 177, 179, 181

koji 17, 19, 21, 23, 33, 36, 39, 55, 67, 115, 117, 119, 121, 123, 173

koshu 36, 47, 87

kura 63, 65, 69, 75, 127, 131, 133, 151, 157, 185, 191, 197

L

lactic acid 123, 175, 177

lactic bacteria 123, 175, 177, 181

lee 23, 43, 57

M

malt 17, 19, 35, 121

mash 19, 23, 41, 57

maturation 23, 47, 69, 73, 129, 133

milling 25, 29, 31, 33, 35, 36, 87, 133, 167

moromi 23

moto 21, 173

multiple parallel fermentation 19

N

nama 67, 69, 71, 73, 75, 79, 97, 161

nama-chozo 73

nama-nama 75

nama-tsume 73

namazake 36, 43, 49, 67, 69, 71, 75, 77, 79, 151

nigori 79, 151, 153, 155, 157, 159, 161

nigorizake 36, 43, 79, 151, 153, 155, 157, 159

nihonshu-do 45, 93, 95, 97, 99, 101

non-distilled beverage 19

non-junmai 36, 39, 41, 55, 59, 107, 117, 119, 125, 133

nurukan 145

O·P·R

o-kan *145*

pasteurized *23, 43, 49, 67, 69, 71, 73, 75, 79*

pressing *57, 153, 155, 157*

regionality *183, 185, 189, 191, 193, 199*

regular (table) sake *39, 41, 45, 55*

S

sakagura *65*

sake brewing *19, 91, 177, 197*

Sake Meter Value *45, 93*

sake rice *27, 29, 33, 165*

seimai-buai *31, 36, 165*

single malt scotch *35*

SMV *92, 93*

sokujo(-moto) *177, 179, 181*

sparkling sake *43*

special designation sake *36, 39*

T

tanrei-karakuchi *195*

tequila *35*

toji *29, 179, 187, 189, 191, 195*

tokubetsu *36, 163, 165, 167, 169, 171*

tokubetsu honjozo *36, 163, 165, 169, 171*

tokubetsu junmai *36, 163, 165, 167, 169, 171*

tokutei meishoshu *36, 39*

Tsuki no Katsura *155, 157*

U·V·Y

unpasteurized *97*

vegan *115, 121, 123, 125*

vintage *89*

Yamada Nishiki *191*

Yamahai *43, 143, 173, 175, 177, 179, 181*

yeast *17, 19, 21, 23, 117, 175, 177, 179, 181*

yeast starter *23, 43, 173, 175, 179*

あ

アスペルギルス・オリーゼ　*18, 116*

温めるか、冷やすか　*136*

熱燗　*144*

アル添　*58, 60, 62, 64*

ヴィンテージ　*88*

お燗　*144*

か

香り　*8, 16, 20, 24, 28, 40, 46, 48, 50, 56, 60, 62, 68, 70, 76, 96, 102, 106, 108, 120, 132, 136, 158*

粕　*22, 42, 56, 114, 152, 156*

燗酒　*144, 146*

貴醸酒　*42*

生酛　*42, 142, 172, 174, 176, 180*

吟醸　*20, 24, 34, 38, 40, 46, 48, 58, 60, 64, 96, 104, 106, 108, 110, 112, 116, 136, 138, 140, 142, 146, 158, 162, 164, 168, 170, 192, 196*

吟醸にごり　*158*

蔵　*62, 64, 68, 74, 126, 128, 132, 150, 156, 186, 190, 196*

グルテン　*114, 116, 118, 120, 122, 124*

原酒　*16, 42*

麹（菌）　*16, 18, 20, 22, 32, 38, 54, 66, 114, 116, 118, 120, 122, 172*

酵素　*16, 18, 38, 66*

酵素菌　*20*

酵母　*16, 18, 20, 22, 116, 174, 176, 178, 180*

古酒　*42, 46, 80, 82, 84, 86, 88, 90*

さ

酒蔵　*64, 80, 82, 84, 88, 98, 108, 110, 118, 122, 126, 128, 130, 150, 154, 156, 162, 166, 168, 170, 176, 180, 186, 188, 190, 192, 194, 196*

酒米　*26, 28, 32, 164*

サケ・メーター・バリュー　*44, 92*

しぼり　*152*

熟成　*22, 42, 46, 48, 68, 72, 80, 82, 84, 86, 88, 90, 128, 130, 132, 134, 184*

熟成温度　*184*

酒母　*20, 22, 42, 172, 174, 178, 180*

純植物性　*114, 120, 122, 124*

純米　*34, 38, 40, 54, 56, 58, 60, 62, 64, 86, 106, 108, 116, 118, 122, 124, 132, 164, 166, 168*

純米吟醸　*34, 38, 58, 64, 106, 122, 162, 166, 168*

純米大吟醸　*34, 38, 58, 64, 106, 122*

純米山廃　*180*

上漕　*152, 156*

醸造 *18, 30, 34, 40, 60, 72, 82, 84, 86, 88, 90, 98, 114, 116, 122, 126, 130, 176, 178, 184, 190, 196*

醸造温度 *184*

醸造業者 *6, 64, 90*

醸造好適米 *164*

醸造者 *28, 178, 186*

醸造酒 *16*

醸造年度 *88*

蒸留アルコール *38, 40, 54, 60, 116*

蒸留酒 *16, 18*

シングル・モルト・スコッチ *34*

精米 *20, 24, 28, 30, 32*

精米歩合 *30, 34, 62, 86, 106, 132, 164, 166, 170*

速醸(酛) *176, 178, 180*

た

大吟醸 *34, 38, 40, 58, 60, 86, 106, 108, 112, 116, 132, 164, 170, 180, 190*

単発酵酒 *16*

淡麗辛口 *194*

地域性 *182, 184, 188, 190, 192, 198*

長期熟成酒 *42, 88, 142*

月の桂 *154, 156*

低温殺菌 *22, 42, 48, 66, 68, 72, 74, 78, 96*

テキーラ *34*

等級 *34, 54, 56, 58, 106, 108, 158, 162, 164, 170, 180*

杜氏 *28, 60, 62, 74, 110, 128, 146, 156, 170, 172, 174, 178, 186, 190*

杜氏組合 *186, 188, 194*

特定名称酒 *38*

特別酒 *162, 164, 166, 170*

特別純米 *162, 164, 166, 168*

特別本醸造 *162, 164, 168*

な

生 *66, 68, 70, 72, 74, 78, 96, 160*

生酒 *42, 48, 66, 68, 70, 74, 76, 78, 150*

生貯蔵 *72*

生詰め *72*

生生 *74*

にごり *78, 150, 152, 154, 156, 158, 160*

にごり酒 *42, 78, 150, 152, 154, 156, 158*

日本酒度 *44, 92, 94, 96, 98, 100*

乳酸 *122, 174, 176*

乳酸菌 *122, 174, 176, 180*

ぬか *18*

ぬる燗 *144*

は

発酵 *16, 18, 22, 28, 32, 40, 56, 58, 116, 150, 174*

発泡日本酒 *42*

火落ち *76*

非蒸留酒 *18*

冷やおろし *72*

風味 *16, 48, 120, 142*

普通酒 *38, 40, 54, 56, 58, 110, 116, 118, 120, 124, 180, 192*

並行複発酵 *18*

本醸造 *34, 40, 58, 108, 110, 116, 162, 168*

本醸造酒 *34, 58, 108, 110, 162*

本生 *74*

ま

酛 *20, 172*

醪 *18, 22, 40, 56*

や

山田錦 *190*

山廃 *172, 174, 176, 178, 180*

E-CAT

English **C**onversational **A**bility **T**est
国際英語会話能力検定

- **E-CATとは…**
  英語が話せるようになるための
  テストです。インターネット
  ベースで、30分であなたの発
  話力をチェックします。

  www.ecatexam.com

iTEP

- **iTEPとは…**
  世界各国の企業、政府機関、アメリカの大学
  300校以上が、英語能力判定テストとして採用。
  オンラインによる90分のテストで文法、リー
  ディング、リスニング、ライティング、スピー
  キングの5技能をスコア化。iTEP®は、留学、就
  職、海外赴任などに必要な、世界に通用する英
  語力を総合的に評価する画期的なテストです。

  www.itepexamjapan.com

[対訳ニッポン双書]
日本の酒
SAKE

2014年11月7日　第1刷発行
2024年3月9日　第5刷発行

著　者　　ジョン・ゴントナー

訳　者　　牛原　眞弓

発行者　　浦　晋亮

発行所　　IBCパブリッシング株式会社
　　　　　〒162-0804 東京都新宿区中里町29番3号 菱秀神楽坂ビル
　　　　　Tel. 03-3513-4511　Fax. 03-3513-4512
　　　　　www.ibcpub.co.jp

印刷所　　株式会社シナノパブリッシングプレス

© John Gauntner 2014
© IBC パブリッシング 2014
Printed in Japan

落丁本・乱丁本は、小社宛にお送りください。送料小社負担にてお取り替えいたします。
本書の無断複写（コピー）は著作権法上での例外を除き禁じられています。

ISBN978-4-7946-0308-1